I0047841

THE BANKABLE SOE
COMMERCIAL FINANCING FOR STATE-OWNED ENTERPRISES

SEPTEMBER 2021

ADB

ASIAN DEVELOPMENT BANK

Creative Commons Attribution 3.0 IGO license (CC BY 3.0 IGO)

© 2021 Asian Development Bank
6 ADB Avenue, Mandaluyong City, 1550 Metro Manila, Philippines
Tel +63 2 8632 4444; Fax +63 2 8636 2444
www.adb.org

Some rights reserved. Published in 2021.

ISBN 978-92-9269-012-0 (print), 978-92-9269-013-7 (electronic), 978-92-9269-014-4 (ebook)
Publication Stock No. TCS210329
DOI: http://dx.doi.org/10.22617/TCS210329

The views expressed in this publication are those of the authors and do not necessarily reflect the views and policies of the Asian Development Bank (ADB) or its Board of Governors or the governments they represent.

ADB does not guarantee the accuracy of the data included in this publication and accepts no responsibility for any consequence of their use. The mention of specific companies or products of manufacturers does not imply that they are endorsed or recommended by ADB in preference to others of a similar nature that are not mentioned.

By making any designation of or reference to a particular territory or geographic area, or by using the term "country" in this document, ADB does not intend to make any judgments as to the legal or other status of any territory or area.

This work is available under the Creative Commons Attribution 3.0 IGO license (CC BY 3.0 IGO) https://creativecommons.org/licenses/by/3.0/igo/. By using the content of this publication, you agree to be bound by the terms of this license. For attribution, translations, adaptations, and permissions, please read the provisions and terms of use at https://www.adb.org/terms-use#openaccess.

This CC license does not apply to non-ADB copyright materials in this publication. If the material is attributed to another source, please contact the copyright owner or publisher of that source for permission to reproduce it. ADB cannot be held liable for any claims that arise as a result of your use of the material.

Please contact pubsmarketing@adb.org if you have questions or comments with respect to content, or if you wish to obtain copyright permission for your intended use that does not fall within these terms, or for permission to use the ADB logo.

Corrigenda to ADB publications may be found at http://www.adb.org/publications/corrigenda.

Notes:
In this publication, "$" refers to United States dollars.
ADB recognizes "China" as the People's Republic of China, "Korea" as the Republic of Korea, and "Vietnam" as Viet Nam.

On the cover: Various state-owned enterprises in ADB's member countries (photos by ADB).

Cover design by Michael Cores.

Contents

Tables and Figures

Foreword

Supporting state-owned enterprise (SOE) reform and seeking to make SOEs "bankable" are long-standing goals of the Asian Development Bank (ADB). Under Strategy 2030, ADB is to promote SOE reform to help "access financing on commercial terms and conditions" and in "attracting private investors and bringing in commercial cofinanciers." The Operational Plans for Strengthening Governance and Institutional Capacity and Private Sector Operations further detail and strengthen ADB's commitment to the promotion of SOE bankability.

This continued commitment reflects the importance of SOEs in ADB's developing member countries. Whether it is in electricity or waste management, water or rural finance, air and sea ports or city subways, SOEs still often play a dominant role. And they have become more bankable. As detailed in this publication, hundreds of SOEs are now listed on the world's stock exchanges and are worth trillions. SOEs have also issued over a trillion in United States dollars in bonds, and they are accessing more and more credit from both local financial institutions and multilateral development banks, including ADB's Public Sector Operations Department (PSOD).

There are three primary advantages of SOEs using commercial financing. Unlike debt with a sovereign guarantee, commercial or nonsovereign borrowing does not add to the public debt and hence limit the government's "fiscal space," allowing the government to borrow for other purposes. This in turn points to the second benefit: the SOE gains the ability to finance investments on its own, and a bankable one should be able to finance more investment in the process. Finally, bankability is an important catalyst for reform: it requires financial sustainability and acceptable levels of transparency and corporate governance. To realize these benefits, the reform must be credible. The expectation that the government will bail out the SOE will undermine reform and create contingent liabilities that limit fiscal space.

To make SOEs bankable, ADB has launched several "One ADB" projects that bring together PSOD with ADB's regional departments that lead our engagement on sovereign projects. These involve substantial capacity building and combine either technical assistance or concessional lending with commercial nonsovereign lending. Examples include Shenzhen Water Climate-Resilient and Smart Urban Water Infrastructure Project (People's Republic of China) and Bengaluru Smart Energy Efficient Power Distribution Project (India).

This work, however, has also been challenging, and that's why this study is so timely. It draws on a range of international good practice and provides several practical tips on how to improve SOE credit worthiness and governance to make them bankable. While of interest to a range of audiences, the primary focus is for SOE leaders and government owners and policy makers who wish to move to commercial financing.

The Bankable SOE is part of ADB's wider effort to promote SOE reform in its developing member countries. Each year, ADB works with a number of state-owned utilities, banks, and other SOEs, where the government does provide a sovereign guarantee, and in all these projects, SOE reform is expected and required. ADB also supports broader sector and national SOE reforms through policy-based lending and technical assistance. The SOE Working Group helps lead and coordinate this work, and *The Bankable SOE* is one of a series of publications and capacity-building activities being carried out under ADB's auspices to promote SOE reform in Asia and the Pacific.

Bruno Carrasco
Director General concurrently
Chief Compliance Officer,
Sustainable Development
and Climate Change Department
Asian Development Bank

Acknowledgments

This study was prepared by William Mako, Asian Development Bank (ADB) consultant, under the supervision of David Robinett, Senior Public Management Specialist (state-owned enterprise reforms). Governance Thematic Group, Sustainable Development and Climate Change Department, ADB, and ADB's State-Owned Enterprise Working Group. The authors would like to thank the following people for their helpful comments and insights: Yurendra Basnett, Senior Public Management Specialist, Southeast Asia Department (SERD); Zheng Hao Chan, Counsel, Office of the General Counsel; Peter Ho, Principal Risk Management Specialist, Office of Risk Management (ORM); Srinivasan Janardanam, Principal Financial Management Specialist, Procurement, Portfolio, and Financial Management Department (PPFD); Donald Lambert, Principal Private Sector Development Specialist, SERD; Hans van Rijn, Principal Public Management Specialist, East Asia Department (EARD), Craig Lee Roberts, Senior Advisor, Private Sector Operations Department (PSOD).

Abbreviations

ADB	Asian Development Bank
BAA	British Airports Authority
BOD	board of director
CAPEX	capital expenditures
CEO	chief executive officer
CGDF	corporate governance development framework
COSO	Committee of Sponsoring Organization
CPSE	central public sector enterprises
DFI	development finance institution
EBIT	earnings before interest and taxes
EBITDA	earnings before interest, taxes, depreciation, and amortization
EBRD	European Bank for Reconstruction and Development
EU	European Union
EVA	economic value-added
FFO	funds flow from operations
FMV	fair market value
GDP	gross domestic product
IAS	International Accounting Standards
ICR	interest coverage ratio
IFC	International Finance Corporation
IFRS	International Financial Reporting Standards
IMF	International Monetary Fund
MDB	multilateral development bank
NCA	non-commercial assistance
NOPAT	net operating profits after tax
OECD	Organisation for Economic Co-operation and Development
PRC	People's Republic of China
PSOD	Private Sector Operations Department
ROE	return on equity

RPT	related-party transactions
SAA	South African Airways
SOE	state-owned enterprise
TPP	Trans-Pacific Partnership
UK	United Kingdom
US	United States

I. Summary

"The Bankable SOE" refers to a state-owned enterprise (SOE) that can borrow from commercial lenders on commercial terms, or has nonstate shareholders, or both.[1] Commercial debt and equity financing offer important advantages, including more fiscal headroom for governments to finance other public needs, greater incentives for productivity, and more market supervision of SOEs to supplement government capacity.

Commercial debt and equity financing of bankable SOEs has become commonplace, as discussed in Section II. By end-2015, at least 800 SOEs with a combined market value of at least $5.3 trillion were listed on major stock exchanges in Organisation for Economic Co-operation and Development (OECD), as well as some non-OECD countries. In emerging markets alone, commercial debt of SOE has likely approached $1.4 trillion.

However, commercial financing can have undesirable outcomes, as discussed in Section III. SOEs experience financial distress. Government rescues may create moral hazard and, in some cases, hurt private sector competitors.

A discussion of risk measurement, sources, and mitigants in Section IV draws on methodologies from international credit rating agencies. Indeed, a key recommendation is that an SOE seeking to access or improve its access to commercial debt or equity financing should work toward an appropriate investment-grade credit rating. Consideration of key risks suggests two prominent groups of potential issues: first, to reduce the country risk, host governments should reduce any differential treatment of SOEs (either positive or negative), and require full and transparent compensation (by either government or SOE) for any residual differential treatment. Key recommendations are summarized in the Appendix.

This study is oriented toward SOE shareholders, boards, and managements. It is *not* an attempt to teach investors how to invest in SOEs. Nor is it a substitute for ratings from international credit rating agencies or a do-it-yourself ratings guide. The Appendix on Suggested Guidelines for Assessing Risk in the Commercial Financing of State-Owned Enterprises seeks only to inform governments and SOE shareholders, boards, and management on possible improvements to obtain commercial finance on more favorable terms while protecting the economy from distress or distortion.

---

[1] SOEs are legal entities established to undertake commercial activities, and owned largely or fully by the sovereign. In practice, this may be through either direct or indirect ownership, and by a national, provincial, or local government or governments. Bankable SOEs will normally have legal forms similar to private sector enterprises.

II. Trends

Two decades ago, the financing of SOEs via direct transfers from national treasuries or directed credits from state banks was common, and heavily criticized. Direct and indirect government funding led to soft-budget constraints and kept SOEs in business that should otherwise be restructured or allowed to go bankrupt.[2]

Since then, nonsovereign debt and equity financing of SOEs has become more common.[3] By end-2015, about 800 SOEs with a combined market value of $5.3 trillion were listed on 31 major public stock exchanges in the OECD and non-OECD countries.[4] These SOEs may have been listed for any number of reasons, including incomplete privatization programs, government nationalizations of distressed private companies, or government desires for access to capital market financing and market supervision. These SOEs are subject to some degree of monitoring and supervision by regulators, stock exchanges, and public shareholders.[5]

In emerging markets, commercial SOE debt is likely approaching $1.4 trillion. Leaving aside bank loans, the emerging market corporate bond market has nearly quadrupled in the past decade to about $2.3 trillion.[6] SOEs account for about 60% of emerging-market non-financial corporate debt—recently standing at 87% in South Africa, 86% in the People's Republic of China (PRC), 80% in Malaysia, 65% in India, 56% in the Russian Federation, 54% in Brazil, 22% in Indonesia, and 21% in Turkey.[7]

Among OECD countries, non-guaranteed SOE debt financing is common. SOEs borrow from commercial lenders in most OECD countries. Among almost half of the OECD countries surveyed, government guarantees on SOE commercial debt are precluded.[8]

Commercial financing of SOEs offers more than just financing. Commercial finance can also encourage SOE boards and management to become more commercially oriented, insulate them from government influence, and generally enhance their corporate governance.

---

[2] W. L. Megginson and J. M. Netter. 2001. *From State to Market: A Survey of Empirical Results on Privatization* (31 August 2001 draft), p. 10. https://www.oecd.org/daf/ca/corporategovernanceofstate-ownedenterprises/1929649.pdf

[3] In nonsovereign finance, lenders or equity investors typically do not have recourse to recovery via any sovereign guarantee in the event of default or loss of value.

[4] OECD. 2017. *The Size and Sectoral Distribution of State-Owned Enterprises.* Paris: OECD Publishing. pp. 27–30. http://dx.doi.org/10.1787/9789264280663-en. There are at least 90 additional exchanges worldwide—including in the Russian Federation, Turkey, Thailand, and South Africa (https://en.wikipedia.org/wiki/List_of_stock_exchanges, accessed 19 April 2021)—on which SOE shares could also be listed.

[5] Throughout this study, "public shareholder" designates a private individual or private company owning shares in a corporation listed on a public stock exchange. "Public company" designates a corporation listed on a public stock exchange. It may be privately owned by public shareholders or of mixed ownership by both public shareholders and a state shareholder(s).

[6] C. Smith and R. Wigglesworth. 2020. Boom in Emerging Market Corporate Debt Stirs Fears. *Financial Times.* 19 January. https://www.ft.com/content/3008bbf6-3878-11ea-a6d3-9a26f8c3cba4

[7] M. Jamrisko, A. Nag, and K. Salna. 2020. Emerging-Market Debt Crisis Brews as State Firms Need Rescue. *Bloomberg* 11 June. https://www.bloomberg.com/news/articles/2020-06-11/rescuing-state-owned-firms-adds-to-emerging-market-debt-crisis

[8] OECD. 2018. *Ownership and Governance of State-Owned Enterprises: A Compendium of National Practices.* Paris: OECD Publishing. pp. 53, 55. https://www.oecd.org/corporate/Ownership-and-Governance-of-State-Owned-Enterprises-A-Compendium-of-National-Practices.pdf

Commercial financing of SOEs by multilateral development banks (MDBs) may be increasing. In emerging market and developing countries, SOEs committed $270 billion for infrastructure investment in 2017, with an additional $130 billion from public entities, for a combined $400 billion of SOE and public entity infrastructure investment. This included $164 billion of debt financing: $118 billion from MDBs, $28 billion from public banks, and $18 billion from commercial banks.[9] It is reasonable to assume that the commercial bank lending and some MDB lending was for SOEs on a nonsovereign basis. At the ADB, the five-year average annual nonsovereign commitments almost tripled from $882 million as of 2011 to $2,361 million as of 2019 (Figure 1). SOEs accounted for 11 of 13 nonsovereign public sector loans during 2006–2011.[10] At the European Bank for Reconstruction and Development (EBRD), "SOE projects are a noteworthy percentage of the EBRD's Power and Energy and Transport portfolios."[11]

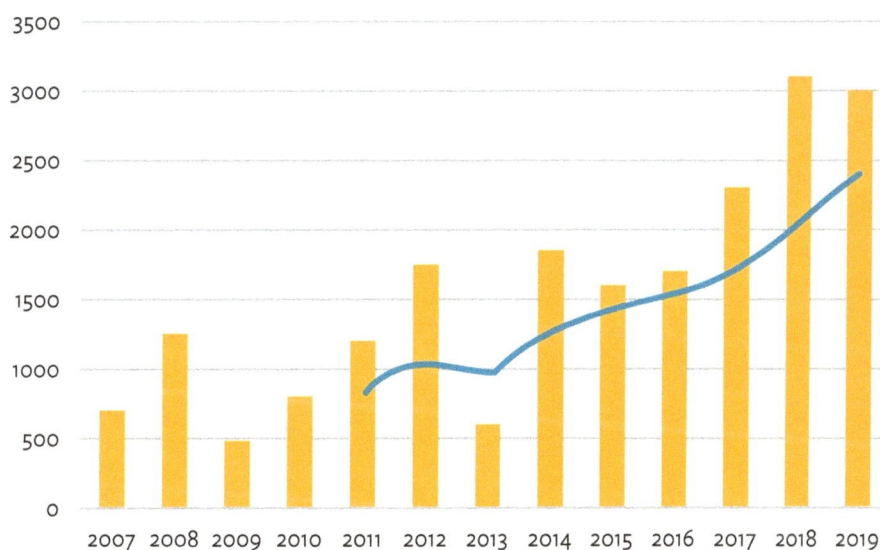

**Figure 1: ADB Nonsoverign Commitment,
Annual and 5-Year Annual Averages, 2007–2019**
($ million)

Source: ADB. 2019. *Asian Development Bank Financial Report, 2019.* Manila.

Further increases in commercial nonsovereign debt or equity financing of SOEs seem likely:
- Developing country needs for investment in public health, primary education, climate change mitigation, and infrastructure are vast. Developing Asia will need to invest an estimated $26 trillion just in infrastructure during 2016–2030 "to maintain its growth momentum, tackle poverty, and respond to climate change."[12]
- Coronavirus disease has reduced fiscal space for many governments, and growing demands from the public sector could outpace increases in MDBs' capital and lending capacity. The implication is that governments need to obtain higher proportions of needed financing commercially on nonsovereign terms.

---

9   Public-Private Infrastructure Advisory Facility (PPIAF). 2017. *Who Sponsors Infrastructure Projects? Disentangling Public and Private Contributions.* Washington, DC: World Bank. pp. 2, 7. https://ppi.worldbank.org/content/dam/PPI/documents/SPIReport_2017_small_interactive.pdf
10   ADB. 2011. Mainstreaming Nonsovereign Public Sector Financing. *Policy Paper.* 23 August. p. 23.
11   EBRD Evaluation Department. 2016. *Transactions with State-Owned Enterprises.* Special Study. p. 6.
12   ADB. 2017. *Meeting Asia's Infrastructure Needs.* Manila: ADB. p. 43. http://dx.doi.org/10.22617/FLS168388-2

- Eager to free up their borrowing capacity to finance noncommercial needs (e.g., for public health, education, and social protection), governments may increasingly release SOEs to obtain commercial financing with no (or limited) recourse to government guarantees.
- General trends toward commercialization and private sector corporate governance norms are making SOEs more suitable candidates for commercial debt or equity funding.
- In addition to seeking capital market funding for SOEs, some governments may welcome the resulting capital market supervision to further improve the corporate governance and efficiency of their SOEs.

A final indication of the frequency of nonsovereign financing is the frequency with which SOEs experience financial distress, as surveyed in Section III.

III.   What Could Go Wrong?

Commercially financed SOEs pose two broad issues for financial markets:

- First, SOE financial distress may cause financial loss to commercial lenders and/or equity investors that, if sufficiently severe, could threaten the financial system;
- Second, government interventions to rescue or promote SOEs may distort investment decisions and financial markets.

A.   Financial Distress

SOE financial distress happens often enough, both in Asia and elsewhere, to pose significant risks to investors:

- An SOE may default by failing to make debt payments on time. For example, in the PRC, SOEs defaulted on 79.5 billion yuan ($12.1 billion) of bonds in 2020."[13] In Viet Nam, the Vinashin state shipbuilding group defaulted on a $600 million syndicated loan to international lenders in 2010.[14]
- Although relatively infrequent, an SOE may be forced into a court-supervised bankruptcy process. For example, after losing money for a decade, South African Airways (SAA) filed for court-supervised "business rescue" in December 2019.[15] In post-transition Latvia and Lithuania, bankruptcy proceedings had been initiated against 290 SOEs by mid-2016.[16]
- Creditors may be forced to accept a restructuring of SOE debt as an alternative to default or bankruptcy. For example, after becoming "the biggest dollar bond defaulter among the nation's state-owned companies in two decades" in December 2019, a Chinese commodities conglomerate announced that holders of $712.5 million of its bonds had accepted 33% to 67% losses in a debt restructuring.[17] In January 2021, Malaysia Airlines posed creditors with a choice between "haircuts" on $4 billion of debt or liquidation of the company.[18]
- SOE financial losses may force a government rescue, either one time or ongoing. For example, having injected over 5 billion ringgit ($1.6 billion) into Malaysia Airlines during the prior decade, the shareholding fund committed an additional 1.4 billion ringgit ($436 million) in August 2014 to buy the remaining 31% of privately

13   R. Frost. 2021. China Huarong Showdown Reveals Beijing's Tougher Stance on Risk. *Bloomberg.* 14 April. https://www.bloomberg.com/news/articles/2021-04-14/china-huarong-showdown-reveals-beijing-s-tougher-stance-on-risk

14   J. Hookway and A. Tudor. 2010. Behind Firm's Default: Vietnam's Growth Mania. *Wall Street Journal.* 25 December. https://www.wsj.com/articles/SB10001424052970203568004576043180815719282

15   P. Vecchiato and A. Squazzin. South African Airways to Enter into Bankruptcy Protection. *Bloomberg.* 4 December. https://www.bloomberg.com/news/articles/2019-12-04/south-african-airways-to-be-placed-into-business-rescue

16   J. Mackevicius, R. Sneidere, and D. Tamuleviciene. 2018. The Waves of Enterprise Bankruptcy and the Factors That Determine Them: The Case of Lithuania and Latvia. *The Journal of Entrepreneurship and Sustainability Issues.* 105. https://doi.org.10.9770/jesi.2018.6.1(8); and Lithuanian Shipping Company Liquidation Starts. *Offshore Energy Biz.* 2 June 2016. https://www.offshore-energy.biz/lithuanian-shipping-companys-liquidation-starts/

17   China Suffers Biggest Dollar Bond Default by State-Owned Company in Two Decades. *Bloomberg.* 11 December. https://www.bloomberg.com/news/articles/2019-12-12/most-investors-accept-haircut-in-china-s-tewoo-bond-revamp#:~:text=A%20major%20Chinese%20commodities%20trader,Tewoo%20Group%20Corp

18   Malaysia Airlines Debt Restructuring Nears Completion—Parent Company. *Reuters.* 7 January. https://www.reuters.com/article/us-malaysia-airlines-restructuring/malaysia-airlines-debt-restructuring-nears-completion-parent-company-idUSKBN29C0T0

owned shares to facilitate the airline's restructuring.[19] In South Africa, government support for the Eskom state electricity utility has cumulatively exceeded 9% of the gross domestic product (GDP) during 2008–2019.[20] In India, central public sector enterprises (CPSEs) rely on loans from the government in addition to borrowing from the financial sector and international agencies. Much larger, however, have been government equity injections into CPSEs, which rose to almost 160,000 crore rupees (about $23.5 billion) by 2016.[21]

SOE financial distress typically results from adverse business or financial circumstances and/or inappropriate management decisions and failures of risk management and risk reporting.[22] Such dangers became obvious in the case of Viet Nam's Vinashin state shipbuilding group, which defaulted in 2010 after a decade of wild growth and debt-fueled expansion into unfamiliar sectors.[23]

Complex corporate and ownership structures cause problems. For example, an analysis of defaults on onshore and offshore bonds by 26 SOEs in the PRC places some blame on sectoral overcapacity and lack of commercialization. However, it also cites the complexity of ownership structures, the SOE parent's capacity for providing financial support, and the ownership "distance" between the defaulting SOE and its ultimate "parent" owner. In more than half of the cases where the defaulting enterprise was majority state-owned, the enterprises were subsidiaries "several layers of ownership away from their ultimate state parent." In addition, "the state parent's capacity to extend support is important. Many of the defaults involved firms with state parents that may not have had adequate resources to bail out distressed subsidiaries."[24]

Internal fraud or corruption and weak corporate governance may exacerbate problems. For example, in the Vinashin case, the CEO and eight other executives were sentenced to 3–20 years in jail for misusing state property and other violations.[25] In South Africa, weak corporate governance and corruption have contributed to Eskom's distress,[26] while a judge in the SAA bankruptcy case found that SAA's chair "blocked, delayed and obstructed important initiatives to turn the airline around. She broke the law and flouted basic governance principles."[27]

Inadequate national frameworks or practices can also exacerbate SOE distress. This may include weak regulation and supervision of financial institutions, including those owned by the state. Especially if related to SOEs, state banks may have little or no incentive to make an objective assessment of SOE lending risk. Indeed, SOEs sometimes

19   A.-Z. A. Hamzah and Y. Ngui. 2014. State Fund to Take Over Malaysia Airlines, Plans "Complete Overhaul." *Reuters.* 7 August. https://www.reuters.com/article/us-malaysia-airline/state-fund-to-take-over-malaysia-airlines-plans-complete-overhaul-idUSKBN0G807E20140808

20   International Monetary Fund. 2020. *South Africa: Staff Report for the 2019 Article IV Consultation.* Washington, DC: IMF. p. 10.

21   A. Chibber. undated. *India's Public Sector Enterprises: Why the Business of Government Is Not Business.* New Delhi: Federation of Indian Chambers of Commerce & Industry and National Institute of Public Finance and Policy. pp. 10–11.

22   OECD. 2015. *OECD Guidelines on Corporate Governance of State-Owned Enterprises.* Paris: OECD Publishing. p. 64. https://www.oecd-ilibrary.org/governance/oecd-guidelines-on-corporate-governance-of-state-owned-enterprises-2015_9789264244160-en

23   Growing 40% a year during 1997–2007, the Vietnam Shipbuilding Industry Group (Vinashin) expanded aggressively into non-core businesses (e.g., real estate, financial services, tourism, beer), such that it had over 160 subsidiaries by 2010. Its total debt, reported at $4.4 billion in July 2010, was 3x its annual sales and 10x its equity. Joint Donor Report to the *Vietnam Consultative Group.* 2011. *Vietnam Development Report 2012: Market Economy for a Middle-Income Vietnam.* Washington, DC: World Bank. p. 38. "Among other things, Vinashin ran aground over its rapid diversification into a host of sectors in which it had only a passing familiarity, if any at all." J. Hookway. 2012. Vinashin Executive Gets Prison Sentence. *Wall Street Journal.* 2 April. https://www.wsj.com/articles/SB10001424052702303816504577317682973934846

24   F. Wire. 2020. Ownership and Sector Key Factors in China SOE Defaults. *Fitch Ratings.* 30 March. https://www.fitchratings.com/research/corporate-finance/ownership-sector-key-factors-in-china-soe-defaults-30-03-2020#:~:text=These%20are%3A%20sectoral%20overcapacity%2C%20the,from%20the%20ultimate%20state%20parent

25   J. Hookway. *Wall Street Journal.* 2 April 2012.

26   IMF. *South Africa: Staff Report.* p. 10.

27   Finding her a "delinquent director," the judge banned her from further directorships. "She was a director gone rogue. She did not have the slightest consideration for her fiduciary duty to SAA." High Court of South Africa, Gauteng Division, Case 15996/17, 27 March 2020, 4–6 and 180–185, https://www.outa.co.za/web/content/88947

receive "directed credits" from banks at the behest of the government. Local rating agencies may be complicit in assigning inappropriately high credit ratings to SOEs or their creditors.[28]

SOEs may sometimes be required to support a broader national agenda at the expense of SOE profitability. For example:

- Utility tariffs may be capped too low. This may, for instance, preclude an electric company from earning enough to provide an adequate risk-adjusted return to equity investors; service payables or debt to vendors, banks or bondholders; or fund necessary maintenance or capital investment to avoid blackouts. For example, delays in raising electricity tariffs in Pakistan contributed to additional 2018–2019 arrears equivalent to 2% of GDP.[29]
- Other "public service mandates" may require an SOE to support employment or regional development. Excess employment and labors costs often result.[30] Similarly, extension of power transmission and distribution to remote regions could cause financial strain.
- SOEs may be also obliged to support macroeconomic goals through capital investments or retaining employees during an economic recession or purchasing (other) SOEs' shares during a stock market downturn.

Government rescue of a distressed SOE may create other financial risks, including fiscal pressure on the government. Capital contributions to a distressed SOE(s) could, for example, increase the fiscal deficit and government borrowing, reduce the nation's sovereign credit rating, and raise the interest rate on government borrowing.[31]

B.   Market Distortions

Government financial rescues and other support for SOEs can create "moral hazard," distort investment decisions, and hurt competition and competitiveness.

Moral hazard arises when investors assume they can invest heedlessly in the expectation that the government would rescue them in the case of financial distress. Allowing investors to experience loss reduces moral hazard. For example, the 2019 financial restructuring in the PRC that cost bondholders 33%–67% of their investment was seen as reducing moral hazard and investor complacency.[32]

---

[28] For example, a joint IMF-World Bank assessment attributed Viet Nam's 2012 financial distress to "a complex array" of factors, including "interference by central and local authorities on the investment and credit decisions of state-owned enterprises (SOEs) and state owned commercial banks (SOCBs); inadequate governance structures and risk management capacity in these institutions; connected lending in several joint-stock banks (JSBs); weaknesses in financial infrastructure, including poor financial reporting standards; and deficiencies in financial regulation and supervision." World Bank. 2014. *Financial Sector Assessment: Vietnam*. Washington, DC: World Bank. p. 1. http://documents1.worldbank.org/curated/en/216401468329363389/pdf/926180FSAP0P1300PUBLIC00Vietnam0FSA.pdf

[29] International Monetary Fund. 2019. *Pakistan: Request for an Extended Arrangement Under the Extended Fund Facility*. Washington, DC: IMF. p. 6. https://www.imf.org/en/Publications/CR/Issues/2019/07/08/Pakistan-Request-for-an-Extended-Arrangement-Under-the-Extended-Fund-Facility-Press-Release-47092

[30] For example, a survey of 98 state and 1,520 private oil companies finds labor productivity roughly double in the private companies. International Monetary Fund. 2020. State-Owned Enterprises: The Other Government. In *Fiscal Monitor*. Washington, DC: IMF. pp. 52, 54. https://www.imf.org/en/Publications/FM/Issues/2020/04/06/fiscal-monitor-april-2020#Chapter%203 . The ratio of staff to aircraft is 3.2x higher at Pakistan International Airlines, compared with Air France-KLM or Singapore Airlines. F. Mangi. 2021. Airline with 14,000 Staff for 30 Planes to Cut Half Its Workforce. *Bloomberg*. 27 April. https://www.bloombergquint.com/onweb/half-of-jobs-to-be-cut-as-pakistan-s-airline-fights-to-survive

[31] Prior to additional pressure on South Africa's sovereign credit ratings from coronavirus disease Goldman Sachs characterized the state-owned Eskom electricity company as "the biggest single risk to the South African economy." R. Bonorchis and P. Burkhardt. 2017. Goldman Sachs Sees Eskom as Biggest Risk to South African Economy. *Bloomberg*. 22 September. https://www.bloomberg.com/news/articles/2017-09-22/goldman-sachs-sees-eskom-as-biggest-risk-to-s-african-economy

[32] X. Yu. Bond Defaults Reach Once-Safe Corners of Chinese Finance. *Wall Street Journal*. 13 December. https://www.wsj.com/articles/bond-defaults-reach-once-safe-corners-of-chinese-finance-11576232065

Moral hazard is an issuing facing SOE financing worldwide. For example, an IMF-World Bank assessment of Indonesia recently found that corporate bond investors often believed SOEs had implicit state support.[33] Among OECD countries, about 40% of survey respondents report that commercial lenders perceive a lower risk for SOE lending, and that preferential terms for commercial lending to SOEs are likely. This occurs even in economies where government guarantees of SOE debt are prohibited (e.g., Estonia, Ireland, Sweden, and Italy).[34] The implication is that commercial lenders believe that—regardless of any rules on government guarantees—in a crisis the government will intervene in support of a financially distressed SOE.

Expectations of government rescue lower SOE funding costs and distort competition. A survey of economies indicates that, on average, SOEs enjoy interest rate discounts of 1.1 percentage points in the 28 developed and 1.4 percentage points in the 37 emerging or developing economies.[35] Lower financing costs can make it easier for SOEs to compete with private firms, encourage additional borrowing and investment in marginal projects, and facilitate other SOE inefficiencies.

Other differences in government treatment of SOEs may also hurt "competitive neutrality." Competitive neutrality between private and publicly owned enterprises is important for efficiency throughout a national economy.[36] An otherwise competitive private enterprise should not be "crowded out" of the market by an SOE whose competitive advantage depends on SOE-specific regulation, taxation, or public procurement practices. But neither should an SOE be competitively disadvantaged by burdensome public policy mandates to support a government's economic or social goals. Potential challenges to competitive neutrality from regulation, taxation, procurement, financing, and compensation mechanisms are discussed further in Section IV.C.

---

[33]   World Bank. 2017. *Financial Sector Assessment: Republic of Indonesia.* Washington, DC: World Bank. p. 23.

[34]   OECD. *Compendium of National Practices.* p. 53.

[35]   IMF. *State-Owned Enterprises.* p. 51; and author's estimates.

[36]   For more on competitive neutrality, by the leader of the international dialogue on this, see OECD. *Compendium of National Practices.* pp. 43–45.

IV. Risk—Measurement, Sources, and Mitigants

Corporate governance provides the foundation for how an SOE shapes its capacities, conducts its business, and manages risk. In addition, government policies, as well as exogenous economic, market, and political developments, will affect the financial risks borne by its equity and debt investors (Figure 2). After summarizing methods for assessing financial risk, this section discusses business or financial decisions, country risk, management capacity, and corporate governance.

Figure 2: Financial Distress: Stylized Chain of Causality

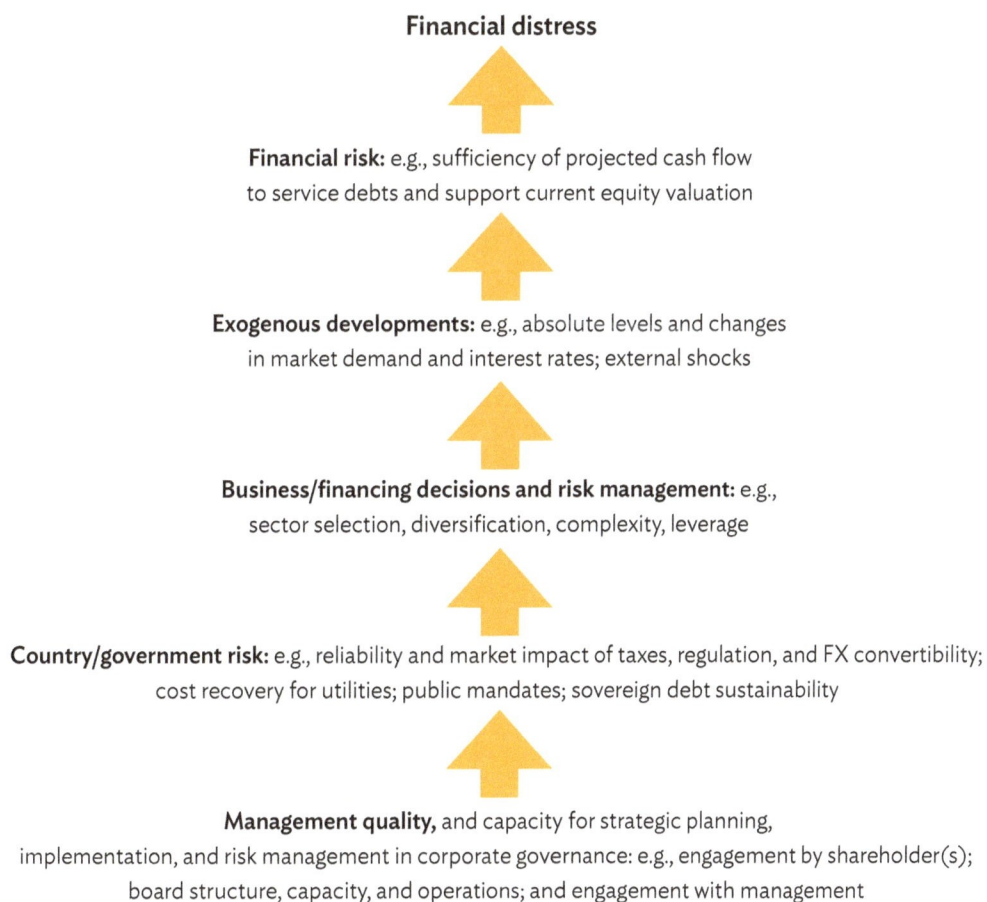

Financial distress

⬆

Financial risk: e.g., sufficiency of projected cash flow to service debts and support current equity valuation

⬆

Exogenous developments: e.g., absolute levels and changes in market demand and interest rates; external shocks

⬆

Business/financing decisions and risk management: e.g., sector selection, diversification, complexity, leverage

⬆

Country/government risk: e.g., reliability and market impact of taxes, regulation, and FX convertibility; cost recovery for utilities; public mandates; sovereign debt sustainability

⬆

Management quality, and capacity for strategic planning, implementation, and risk management in corporate governance: e.g., engagement by shareholder(s); board structure, capacity, and operations; and engagement with management

Source: Asian Development Bank.

A.   Financial Risk

Creditors and shareholders tend to view financial risk differently:
- Creditors may focus on whether the debtor has sufficient cash flow to service its debt continuing to pay interest and repaying principal when due.
- Shareholders may focus on dividends and/or market value. The latter is closely linked to dividend payments or return on equity (ROE) depending on the sector. In addition, shareholders are sensitive to any "credit event" that could diminish or eliminate their equity returns.[37]

Credit rating agencies are skeptical of ratios based just on accounting-based "book values," for example, debt-to-equity. Such book value-based ratios "do not always reflect current market values or the ability of the asset base to generate cash flow to service debt."[38]

Table 1: Definitions of Cash Flow and Cash Flow Proxies

	Revenues
-	Operating expenditure
+	Depreciation and amortization
=	**Earnings before Interest, Taxes, Depreciation, and Amortization (EBITDA)**
+/-	Recurring dividends received from associates, less cash dividends paid to minority interests
-	Cash interest paid and net of interest received
-	Cash tax paid
-	Long-term rentals
=	**FFO**
=/-	Changes in working capital (e.g., receivables, inventory, payables)
=	CFO
+/-	Non-operational cash flow
-	Capital expenditure
-	Ordinary dividends paid to shareholders of the parent company
=	**FCF**
=	Receipts from asset disposals
-	Business acquisitions
+	Business divestments
+/-	Exceptional or other cash flow items
=	**Net Cash Flow, in or out**

Source: Adapted from Fitch. *Corporate Rating Criteria.* p. 51.

Instead, credit rating agencies focus more on cash-flow measures. Short of a complete calculation of cash flow for a period, analysts use various cash flow approximations (or proxies) (Table 1). Earnings before interest, taxes, depreciation, and amortization (EBITDA) "is widely used" and "serves as a useful and common starting point for

---

[37]   Credit events include default, forced debt restructuring, insolvency, missed debt service, or violation of lending covenants.
[38]   Fitch Ratings. 2020. *Corporate Rating Criteria.* p. 5. https://www.fitchratings.com/research/corporate-finance/corporate-rating-criteria-21-12-2020

cash flow analysis and . . . ranking the financial strength of different companies," but "has significant limitations."[39] Funds flow from operations (FFOs) is also useful, which adjusts EBITDA for dividends, interest payments, taxes, and long-term rentals.

Comparisons of cash flow proxies with debt or debt service requirements provide some basis for assessing financial resiliency. The ratio of EBITDA to interest expense is an important *short-term* indicator of financial resiliency. If this interest coverage ratio decreases toward or below 1.0, an enterprise's ability to meet its interest expense obligations increasingly comes into doubt. An important limitation is that the interest coverage ratio neglects an enterprise's ability to repay the underlying debt (i.e., the principle).

Even the most relevant financial metrics should not be used in a deterministic fashion, but instead be viewed in the context of sector volatility. Earnings and cash flow volatility vary widely among sectors. For example, among United States companies during 2011–2020, the standard deviation in annual operating income varied from 19% to 34% for a medial range of sectors (e.g., insurance, broadcasting, and healthcare facilities) to a below-medial range of 6%-16% for tobacco, utilities, railroads, and aerospace or defense and an above-medial range of 34% to 154% for basic chemicals, shipbuilding, steel, air transport, mobile telephony, precious metals, and oil or gas.[40] Less subject to earnings swings that could leave it without enough cash flow to service its debt, a low-volatility company can service given leverage more comfortably than can a high-volatility company. According to one set of benchmark ranges (Table 2), for example, for an enterprise of below-medial volatility, FFO at 30% of debt and debt at 3× EBITDA would be assessed as "modest leverage." These would be assessed as "significant leverage," however, for an enterprise of above-medial volatility.

Table 2: Illustrative Benchmark Ranges for Assessing Leverage

Leverage assessment	Earnings volatility	FFO/Debt	Debt/EBITDA
Modest	Below medial	23%–35%	2–3×
	Medial	35%–50%	1.75–2.5×
	Above medial	45%–60%	1.5–2×
Significant	Below medial	9%–13%	4–5×
	Medial	13%–23%	3.5–4.5×
	Above medial	20%–30%	3–4×
High	Below medial	<6%	>6×
	Medial	<9%	>5.5×
	Above medial	<12%	>5×

EBITDA = earnings before interest, taxes, depreciation, and amortization, FFO = funds flow from operations.
Source: Adapted from S&P. *Corporate Methodology*. pp. 33-34.

---

[39] "Because EBITDA derives from income statement entries, it can be distorted by the same accounting issues that limit the use of earnings as a basis of cash flow. In addition, interest can be a substantial cash outflow for speculative-grade companies and therefore EBITDA can materially overstate cash flow in some cases." S&P Global 2018. *Corporate Methodology*. New York: Standard & Poor's Financial Services LLC. p. 69. https://www.spratings.com/scenario-builder-portlet/pdfs/CorporateMethodology.pdf

[40] NYU Stern. Betas by Sector (US). New York: Leonard N. Stern School of Business http://pages.stern.nyu.edu/~adamodar/New_Home_Page/datafile/Betas.html. (accessed 08 August 2021) It seems to be reasonable to assume that absolute deviations would differ, but sectoral volatility would bear a general resemblance in other countries. The text highlights sectors in which SOEs are active globally.

Some additional comments are in order:

Trends in several ratios are often a better indicator than any one ratio.[41]

The importance of particular financial metrics may shift depending on an enterprise's prospects. For example, if a company's outlook deteriorates from speculative to distressed, a rating agency's analytical focus might shift from the company's cash flow to its liquidity and ability to refinance—the latter influenced by asset quality.[42]

Forward projections and historical analyses of cash flow, debt, and interest each have their uses:
- Forward projections are most useful to estimate future debt service capacity and equity value.
- Retrospective analyses are more useful for assessing an enterprise's management and corporate governance.[43] This broader perspective may be of greater interest to equity investors.

Equity investor emphasis on dividends versus market value or ROE will tend to vary by sector:
- Dividends are often more important for mature enterprises and stable sectors, where shareholders may be most interested in whether future cash flows will support steady growth in per-share dividends.
- For a younger and capital-intensive enterprise or one in a more cyclical or volatile sector—discouraging dividends—shareholders may tend to focus on the ability of an enterprise's ROE to support higher share prices. The stock market often rewards rising ROE with increasing price-earnings ratios, further raising the share price.

Financial perspectives will differ the most between creditors and ROE-focused equity investors. Because the ROE percentage will be higher for a given cash flow, the less equity there is in an enterprise's capital structure, such equity investors may favor more debt (leverage) and less equity. Thus, a general difference in preferences for "financial resiliency" among banks or bondholders and "financial efficiency" among shareholders becomes even more pronounced in the case of ROE-oriented equity investors.

Thus, in-sector comparisons are highly relevant. For an SOE, as for any corporation, how do its EBITDA/revenues, EBITDA/interest, dividend payout ratio, dividend yield, ROE, and price-earnings ratio compare with other enterprises in the sector?

Financial risk assessment is too complex, however, to offer simple benchmarks here for an SOE seeking commercial financing on an nonsovereign basis.

Debt and equity investors would be best served by independent and expert ratings of an SOE's creditworthiness. These would ideally come from several international rating agencies. Each such rating agency could draw upon extensive databases of industry conditions, practices, and norms to distinguish among below-average, average, and above-average financial performance and position. Typically, ratings would combine prospective and retrospective analyses, and adjust factor weights depending on prospects for the SOE. A host of other items—for example, corporate complexity, strategic positioning, risk management, country risk, management effectiveness and capacity, and corporate governance—would factor into a corporate debt rating (see Section IV.B–E). The methodologies followed by the main international rating agencies differ somewhat, which enhances the value of ratings from multiple agencies.

The cost of obtaining such credit ratings may be an important consideration. The SOE would have to pay rating agencies' fees, cooperate in sharing information, and provide regular access for these rating agencies to update

---

[41]   Fitch. *Corporate Rating Criteria.* p. 5.
[42]   Fitch. *Corporate Rating Criteria.* pp. 41–42.
[43]   Fitch. *Corporate Rating Criteria.* p. 3.

their rating assessments. A decision to pursue multiple credit ratings should reflect an assessment by the SOE's board that the value of additional and/or cheaper financing more than offsets such ratings-related costs.

An SOE's shareholders should aspire to an "investment grade" rating. This includes an AAA, AA, A, or BBB rating. Higher ratings tend to be associated with lower leverage and lower borrowing costs. A higher proportion of equity in the SOE's capital structure, however, would tend to constrain its ROE. Whether an SOE's equity stakeholders (i.e., shareholders, board of directors [BOD], and management) target a higher rating (e.g., AAA or AA) or one just below that (e.g., A or BBB) would likely reflect the SOE's key characteristics (e.g., mature vs. growth stage, stable vs. cyclical or volatile) and these stakeholders' preferences for financial resiliency versus financial efficiency. Investment grade ratings would tend to facilitate an SOE's access to international capital markets.

Before asking international agencies to rate an SOE's credit for the first time, equity stakeholders might consider additional factors that may affect such ratings. The following discussion (Section IV.B–E) of business or financial decisions and risk management, country and government risk, management capacity, and corporate governance factors can usefully inform SOE shareholders, boards, and managements about areas for improvement before and during engagements with international rating agencies. Key recommendations are summarized in the Appendix.

International capital market access tends to be more challenging for an SOE with below-investment grade ratings. Such an SOE may find fewer parties willing to provide loans or buy its bonds, face substantially higher interest charges, or lack credit access altogether. In its "marginal" column, the Appendix suggests benchmarks for a rating just below investment-grade (e.g., BB). This, however, excludes SOEs considered "highly speculative" (e.g., B+, B, or B- ratings) or "distressed" (e.g., CCC+, CCC, or CCC- ratings). To provide some guidance on how an SOE might progress from "distressed" or "highly speculative" toward "marginal."

B.   Business and/or Financial Decisions and Risk Management

Sectors vary widely in terms of typical returns on investment, capital intensity, and variability in earnings and cash flow available for dividends or reinvestment. These variations reflect other differences: for example, whether a particular sector is growing, mature, declining, or cyclical; the extent of competition and barriers to entry; an enterprise's ability to dominate its market and influence prices; and its comparative cost position.

SOEs may respond to such differences by (i) seeking revenue enhancements or cost efficiencies in an existing business and accepting its sectoral characteristics, or (ii) investing in a new business sector, sometimes in an effort to dampen earnings and cash flow volatility. The second should be approached cautiously.

In general, SOEs should earn a profit on top of their cost of capital, and any investment in a new business should be subject to some rate-of-return target. SOEs may also have "mandates" provided in their founding documents or provided by their shareholder to focus on certain areas, and these mandates should generally be respected. SOE diversification may also crowd out private sector activities in certain areas. Even when SOEs are expected to operate independently from the government as fully commercial entities, diversification must be approached carefully for financial reasons, as discussed in the following section.

Economic value-added (EVA) is a useful concept for assessing the financial performance of any corporation, SOEs included. EVA equals net operating profits after tax (NOPAT), minus capital costs. Capital costs include both interest (i) on the debt (D) and expected return (r) on the equity (E) used to produce these operating profits. Thus,

$$EVA = NOPAT - [(D \times i) + (E \times r)]$$

By contrast, earnings per share "will increase so long as new capital investments earn anything more than the after-tax cost of borrowing." This, as an early advocate of EVA noted, "is hardly an acceptable return."[44]

The expected ROE should depend on the business risk associated with the sector in which the equity is invested. "Risk is the variability or uncertainty in the prospective return," and hence, in the *opportunity cost* of investing equity in a particular sector. Compared with the 1.0 risk of a broad equity index, the S&P500, risk levels have gravitated toward 0.6–0.8 for food companies, 1.2–1.4 for cyclical companies (e.g., steel, cement, aluminum, automotive, and chemical), to 1.5+ for airlines and construction, and to 2.0+ for new companies developing new technologies.[45] Thus, two SOEs with identical capital structures and operating profits could—depending on the riskiness of the sector in which each operates—generate either positive or negative EVA (Table 3).

Table 3: Effect of Sector Risk on EVA: Two Hypothetical SOEs

Sector:	Food	Airlines
Market factors:		
Interest rate on debt	3%	3%
Average equity market return	10%	10%
Sector risk	0.8	1.5
Sector-specific expected equity return	0.10 × 0.8 = 8%	0.10 × 1.5 = 15%
Capital structure:		
Debt	500	500
Equity	500	500
	1,000	1,000
Cost of capital:		
Debt	500 × 0.03 = 15	500 × 0.03 = 15
Equity	500 × 0.08 = 40	500 × 0.15 = 75
	55	90
Operating results:		
Revenues	1,000	1,000
Operating expenses (excluding interest)	−900	−900
Earnings before interest and taxes	100	100
Taxes	−20	−20
NOPAT	80	80
Cost of capital	−55	−90
EVA	25	−10

EVA = economic value-added, NOPAT = net operating profits after tax, SOE = state-owned enterprise.
Source: Asian Development Bank.

[44]   G. Bennett Stewart, III. 1991. *The Quest for Value: The EVA Management Guide.* USA: Harper Collins. pp. 2–3.
[45]   Stewart. *The Quest for Value.* pp. 76–78.

Leading economies have used EVA or other rate-of-return targets to assess SOEs' financial performance. For example, state shareholders in Sweden, Singapore, and the Republic of Korea were using EVA by the early 2000s.[46] It is now being used in many more countries, often combined with sector-specific rate of return targets.[47]

Thus, EVA-oriented analyses of actual SOE performance and prospective returns on new SOE investments, including into a new business sector, would constitute best practice. It is also acceptable to set other return on capital or equity targets, what is most important is to have such a target.

Dividend policy is another useful tool for exerting financial discipline over SOEs. A long-standing literature focuses on principle-agent differences between corporate shareholders and managers, and the need to impose financial discipline to avoid "empire building" and other abuses of "free-cash flow."[48] This tendency to invest or otherwise retain funds and not turn them over to shareholders is ever more pronounced in SOEs.

Among OECD countries, almost two-thirds of those surveyed maintain some type of dividend policy for SOEs.[49] This can include a percentage of net income to be paid out as dividends; but also guidance on profits that should be retained for investment and to avoid excess leverage that would hurt the SOEs credit rating. The benchmark is often dividend payments by comparable private sector companies and ensuring that something is paid to the state shareholder (footnote 47).

The desirability of diversification, by an SOE or any corporation, into new business sectors is debatable.
- Credit rating agencies may rate more highly a corporation with sufficient sector diversification to smooth out its overall cash flow through economic cycles.[50]
- A shareholder focused on the market value of equity, however, might take a more skeptical view of diversification. One study of >1,400 firms found, for example, "that diversified firms are consistently valued less than specialized firms."[51] Stock market histories are replete with examples of "diworseification."[52] SOE diversification campaigns in emerging markets can, as noted earlier, end badly.[53]

Indeed, complex corporate and ownership structures may increase financial risk. A large number of related parties within a corporate group increase the opportunities for related-party transactions (RPTs). RPTs are not necessarily fraudulent. However, management can use RPTs for its personal gain, for example, by selling product below fair market value to a related party for subsequent resale at fair market value; lending at a below-market rate, or without any repayment schedule, or to a related party unable to repay; exchanging property at nonmarket prices; allowing ongoing receivables from related parties; or providing unwarranted consulting opportunities and fees.[54] Alternatively, management can use RPTs to mislead outside shareholders and creditors, for instance, through sham

---

[46] W. P. Mako and C. Zhang. 2002. Exercising Ownership Rights in State Owned Enterprise Groups: What China Can Learn from International Experience. Working Paper 26878. Beijing: World Bank. pp. 12–13. http://documents1.worldbank.org/curated/en/264831468769309943/pdf/268780REV.pdf

[47] OECD. Compendium of National Practices. p. 57.

[48] F. Allen and R. Michaely. Payout Policy. pp. 61–62. https://ssrn.com/abstract=309589 or http://dx.doi.org/10.2139/ssrn.309589

[49] OECD. Compendium of National Practices. p. 53.

[50] S&P Global. Corporate Methodology. pp. 36–37.

[51] L. H. P. Lang and R. M. Stulz. 1994. Tobin's q, Corporate Diversification, and Firm Performance. Journal of Political Economy. 102 (6), pp. 1258, 1278. https://www.jstor.org/stable/2138786

[52] Following summaries of ten unsuccessful corporate diversifiers, a highly successful equity fund manager concludes that "There's a strong tendency for companies that are flush with cash and feeling powerful to overpay for acquisitions, expect too much from them, and then mismanage them." P. Lynch. One Up on Wall Street. New York: Simon & Schuster. pp. 153–157. Among the factors that often result in failed acquisitions, another compilation of case studies includes business and/or deal complexity and acquiring management's biases from "recent successes, sunk costs, pride, [and] over-optimism." R. F. Bruner. 2005. Deals from Hell: M&A Lessons That Rise Above the Ashes. Hoboken, NJ: John Wiley & Sons. p. 9.

[53] For example, see footnote 23.

[54] Fraud and Related Party Transactions. Board and Fraud—A Jonathan T. Marks Blog.

transactions between related subsidiaries.[55] Most RPTs are not fraudulent. However, the potential for mischief from RPTs is high enough to warrant careful scrutiny and to lead at least one rating agency to provide a sub-rating for corporate complexity and treatment of RPTs (Table 4).

Table 4: Illustrative Criteria for Rating Corporate Complexity and Transparency

aa	a	bbb	bb	b	ccc
Transparent group structure	Group structure has some complexity, but mitigated by transparent reporting	Some group complexity leading to somewhat less transparent accounting statements. No significant related-party transactions	Complex group structure or non-transparent ownership structure. Related-party transactions exist, but with reasonable economic rationale	Highly complex group with large and opaque related-party transactions or an opaque ownership structure	Group structure sufficiently complex or compromised (e.g., disputed ownership) to materially impair strategic and financial progress

Source: Fitch. *Corporate Rating Criteria*. 75.

Rating agency criteria for assessing any corporation's strategic positioning and risk management can be directly applied to SOEs (Table 5). Risk management should embrace environmental and social considerations that could pose a financial risk (e.g., from a dam collapse) or a legal or reputational risk (e.g., from mistreatment of workers, competitors, or consumers) to the SOE.

Table 5: Illustrative Criteria for Strategic Positioning and Risk Management

Item	Positive	Neutral	Negative
Strategic positioning:			
1. Strategic planning process	Evidence of strategic plans with specific financial and operational goals, with clear measures of achievement.	Strategic plans lack depth or specific financial or operational goals; achievement measures unclear.	Very limited evidence of strategic plans or superficial planning.
2. Consistency of strategy with organizational capabilities and market conditions	Strategy nearly always consistent with enterprise capabilities, taking into account market conditions; has a track record of market leadership and effective innovation.	Strategy generally consistent with enterprise capabilities, taking into account market conditions.	Strategy inconsistent with enterprise capabilities or market conditions. Abrupt or frequent changes in strategy, acquisitions, divestitures, or restructurings
3. Ability to track, adjust and control strategy implementation	Management has been able to convert nearly all strategic decisions into constructive action; has a track record of achieving financial and or operational goals; and successful relative to peers.	Management has been able to convert most strategic decisions into constructive action; has a track record of achieving most financial and or operational goals.	Management often unable to convert strategic decisions into constructive action; often fails to achieve its financial and or operational goals.
Risk management and financial management:			
4. Comprehensiveness of enterprise-wide risk management standard	Management has successfully instituted comprehensive policies that effectively identify, monitor, select and mitigate key risks, and has articulated tolerances to shareholders.	Management has a basic set of standards and tolerances in place, but may not have fully developed risk management capabilities.	Management has no or few defined standards and tolerances, and little risk management capability.

continued on next page

---

[55] For a clear illustration of how RPTs can be used to deceive outsiders, see D. G. Lee. 2003. The Restructuring of Daewoo. In S. Haggard, W. Lim, and E. Kim, eds. *Economic Crisis and Corporate Restructuring in Korea*. Cambridge, UK: Cambridge University Press. pp. 158–163.

Table 5 *continued*

5.	Standards for operational performance	Management has set rigorous and ambitious (but reasonable) standards for operational performance.	Management has set standards for operational performance that are achievable and similar to industry norms.	Management lacks the wherewithal, discipline, or commitment to achieve set standards, or has low standards.

Source: Adapted from Standard & Poors. 2012. Methodology: Management and Governance Credit Factors for Corporate Entities and Insurers. p. 5.

C.   Country Risk

Country risk encompasses many factors, including economic prospects and resilience, financial sector development, and legal and regulatory environment. These may affect all corporations, or (see Section IV.C.2) just SOEs.

1.   All Corporations

Country risk is considered to have an "asymmetric effect" on corporations:
- A company's rating is not raised because of low country risk.
- Excessive country risk may, however, reduce a corporation's rating below what it would otherwise be on a standalone basis based on the company's own finances, business operations, management and governance. "In emerging markets especially, the operating environment can result in a lower rating profile by one to two notches, depending on the level of challenge posed by that environment." Thus, for example, a higher risk country environment could reduce a corporation's credit rating from BBB (investment grade) to BB+ (below investment grade) (footnote 43).

Sovereign default risk is one aspect of country risk. A corporate credit rating may surpass the sovereign credit rating of its home government. However, this is rare, occurring in less than 3% of ratings.[56] The factors justifying an above-sovereign corporate credit rating could include high foreign exchange reserves or earnings; strong liquidity and capital; a well-documented risk mitigation plan; non-dependence on government revenues; and focus on a sector of "moderate sensitivity" to any government default (e.g., telecommunications, natural resource exports, staple consumer goods).[57]

For broader assessments of overall country risk, methodologies vary. For example:
- Standard & Poors weighs (i) economic risk (affected by income level, growth prospects, economic diversity and volatility, monetary policy, external factors, and economic imbalances); (ii) institutional risk (effectiveness, stability and predictability of policymaking and institutions, as well as statistical coverage and reliability and security risks); (iii) financial sector risk (banking sector, adjusted for the depth of capital market and private sector debt and or GDP); and (iv) rule of law (payment culture, contract enforcement, insolvency system, and expropriation risk).[58]
- Fitch emphasizes economic environment, financial system development, and governance indicators (Table 6). Economic indicators focus on resilience to international economic shocks and the risk of domestic factors

---

[56] For example, of Moody's 2,500 corporate bond ratings, just 65 are rated above the sovereign, of which 50 are only one "notch" higher. J. Mariathasan. 2019. Ratings: When Corporates Can Trump Sovereigns. *IPE Magazine*. March. https://www.ipe.com/ratings-when-corporates-can-trump-sovereigns/10029820.article#:~:text=The%20sovereign%20is%20usually%20the,are%20only%20one%20notch%20

[57] S&P Global. 2018. *Ratings Above the Sovereign—Corporate and Government Ratings: Methodology and Assumptions*. New York: Standard & Poor's Financial Services LLC. pp. 2, 9–11, 19. updated 14 December 2018. https://www.maalot.co.il/Publications/GMT20190225151039.PDF

[58] S&P Global. 2013. *Country Risk Assessment Methodology and Assumptions*. New York: Standard & Poor's Financial Services LLC. pp. 4–8. https://www.spratings.com/scenario-builder-portlet/pdfs/CountryRiskAssessmentMethodologyAssumptions.pdf

(e.g., fiscal deficits, current account deficits, and domestic or foreign debt) that might cause a sovereign default. Financial sector factors assess the risk of a banking or capital market crisis that hurts sovereign and/ or corporate debt service capacity. The financial sector focus on entry barriers indicates concern for limits on financial supervisory capacity and risks of bad lending by market entrants who do not meet "fit and proper" standards.

Table 6: Illustrative Summary Criteria for Country Risk Assessment

	aaa	aa	A	bbb	bb	B	ccc
Economic environment	Highly stable, major advanced economy; very high resilience to economic shocks	Very stable, major advanced economy; high resilience to economic shocks	Stable, major advanced economy; good resilience to economic shocks	Moderately stable economy; could be less advanced, but with fair resilience to economic shocks	Less stable; less advanced economy susceptible to adverse changes in domestic situation or international shocks	Volatile, less advanced economy; highly susceptible to adverse changes in domestic situation or international shocks	Unstable economy; highly susceptible to even moderate changes in domestic or international economic situations
Financial system development	Banking system highly developed and concentrated; very high entry barriers; and highly advanced financial markets	Banking sector very developed and concentrated; high entry barriers; and very advanced financial markets	Banking sector developed and concentrated; meaningful entry barriers; and advanced financial markets	Banking sector less developed or diffuse; only moderate barriers to entry; and financial markets developed but not deep	Banking sector diffuse; only limited entry barriers; and financial markets not fully developed	Banking sector very diffuse; no barrier to entry; and financial markets less developed	Banking sector highly diffuse; no barrier to entry; and financial markets undeveloped
Governance	n.a.	Weighted average of World Bank's worldwide governance indicators in the top 20%	Weighted average of World Bank's worldwide governance indicators in the top 30%	Weighted average of World Bank's worldwide governance indicators in the top 50%	Weighted average of World Bank's worldwide governance indicators in the top 60%	Weighted average of World Bank's worldwide governance indicators in the bottom 40%	n.a.

Source: Fitch. *Corporate Rating Criteria* 70.

Half of this governance sub-assessment for country risk reflects a "rule of law" sub-sub-assessment (Table 7), which measures perceptions of the extent to which economic agents can have confidence in contract enforcement, property rights, and physical security. Another sub-assessment of government effectiveness receives a 20% weight. The remaining 30 % of the governance assessment reflects sub-assessments for (in descending priority) control of corruption, regulatory quality, political stability, voice, and accountability.

Table 7: Worldwide Governance Indicators and Illustrative Weighting

Governance dimensions	Weight	Perceptions measured
Political stability	0.03	• The likelihood of political instability and/or politically motivated violence, including terrorism.
Government effectiveness	0.20	• The quality of public services, the quality of the civil service and the degree of its independence from political pressures, the quality of policy formulation and implementation, and the credibility of the government's commitment to such policies.
Rule of law	0.50	• The extent to which agents have confidence in and abide by the rules of society, and in particular the quality of contract enforcement, property rights, the police, and the courts, as well as the likelihood of crime and violence.
Control of corruption	0.15	• The extent to which public power is exercised for private gain, including both petty and grand forms of corruption, as well as "capture" of the state by elites and private interests.
Voice & accountability	0.02	• The extent to which a country's citizens are able to participate in selecting their government, as well as freedom of expression, freedom of association, and a free media.
Regulatory quality	0.10	• The ability of the government to formulate and implement sound policies and regulations that permit and promote private sector development.
	1.00	

Source: https://info.worldbank.org/governance/wgi/ and Fitch. *Corporate Rating Criteria.* 70. Regulatory quality has replaced the "ease of doing business" dimension cited previously by Fitch.

Improvements in the rule of law (and related ratings) could improve the country ratings for some Asian jurisdictions. On average, Asian countries now place in the middle third of the World Bank's rule-of-law rankings. Following the aforementioned methodology (Table 6), these rule-of-law average percentiles would correspond to "bbb" for East Asia and Pacific and "b" rule-of-law sub-ratings for South Asia.

2.   Specific to State-Owned Enterprises

This study focuses on "the bankable SOE," which is able to obtain commercial financing on investment-grade terms solely on its own business, financial, management, and governance merits. Thus, the fact that SOE standalone credit ratings are sometimes adjusted upwards—to reflect the probability of extraordinary government support in an emergency[59]—is of less relevance here.

SOEs may, however, benefit or suffer from special treatment related solely to their state ownership. This may involve differences in regulation, taxation, public procurement, public service mandates, financial assistance, or compensation for public service mandates or adjustments for special treatment relating to state ownership.

Regulation tends to be identical or similar in advanced economies. However, SOEs are still subject to SOE-specific regulations in some jurisdictions.

---

[59]   For example, an SOE's dependence on and the likelihood of government support might be considered high or very high if more than 10% of its revenues come from government transfers or purchases, if SOE dividends account for more than 10% of government revenue, if the SOE and government both derive >75% of their income from within the government's national territory, and/or both have exposure to common credit risks. Moody's. 2020. *Government-Related Issuers Methodology.* 21 February. New York: Moody's Investors Service, Inc. p. 10. https://www.moodys.com/researchdocumentcontentpage.aspx?docid=PBC_1186207

In 27 of 29 OECD countries, SOEs are mostly treated the same as private sector companies. Some include exemptions from competition law for SOEs operating in natural monopolies or reserved markets (four cases) or limited regulatory preferences or exemptions, including easier access to land and certain approvals. Non-OECD Argentina, South Africa, and the PRC follow a similar pattern, while SOE regulation is reportedly more on a case-by-case basis for OECD member Mexico and non-OECD member the Russian Federation.[60]

Among seven Asian countries, all but a few SOEs are incorporated under the company law in India and Bhutan, and 68 Indian SOEs are listed and subject to the same governance and disclosure rules as listed companies. In the Republic of Korea, Pakistan, and the Philippines, SOEs are a mix of standard companies and specialized corporate forms. In Thailand and Viet Nam, most SOEs come under special legislation or have a special legal status.[61]

Taxation of SOEs also tends to be identical or similar. Among 31 OECD economies, SOEs are taxed the same as the private sector in 20 countries and to "largely similar tax treatment" in seven. SOEs in the PRC and Kazakhstan are "subject to largely similar tax treatment," but with exceptions. SOEs in the Russian Federation's appear to be subject to have a separate tax regime. Common exceptions include the following: (1) SOEs carrying out non-commercial and universal service obligations (e.g., in postal sector), and or (2) entities that are classified as SOEs but are effectively operating as part of the general governments. Over-taxation does not seem to be a problem. "A minority of countries consider their SOEs to be at a tax disadvantage due to higher corporate tax rates or inability to benefit from tax write-offs."[62] In 36 countries, tax treatment has either a neutral effect or may somewhat benefit SOEs.

Like private corporations, SOEs should comply with a wide variety of laws and regulations. These include for tax as well as for anti-money laundering, antitrust and competition, privacy, environmental protection, health and safety, anti-fraud and corruption, labor, licensing, and trade. Violation could result in legal sanctions (e.g., fines and imprisonment), financial costs (e.g., reductions in revenues, share price, or investor confidence), business disruption, or reputational harm.[63] Thus, even an SOE rated as "marginal" (as shown in the Appendix) should comply with regulatory, tax, or legal obligations and maintain stable relations with the relevant government authorities.

Public procurement from SOEs can pose competition issues. Large and well-established SOEs may enjoy competitive advantages that a potential market entrant would find difficult or impossible to overcome. Thus, some OECD governments have implemented rules on the conditions under which SOEs may act as suppliers to the government and how SOEs will be treated in public tenders. "For example, in Australia government businesses must declare that their tenders are compliant with competitive neutrality principles; whereas in Sweden, abnormally low tenders can be excluded when they are a result of competitive advantages emanating from government ownership or support."[64]

Public service mandates can hurt SOE profitability. Governments may require SOEs to provide goods or services (e.g., electricity) too cheaply, or otherwise pay to support the government's regional development, employment, or other macroeconomic goals. Utilities can be considered a special case.

In many cases, utilities (e.g., electricity) must provide services below their full cost. This is often motivated by a government's desire to provide a general social benefit or protect vulnerable populations. A survey of 24 electric

---

60   OECD. *Compendium of National Practices.* pp. 45–46. See actual report for additional detail.

61   OECD. 2018. *Managing Risk in the State-Owned Enterprise Sector of Asia: Stocktaking of National Practices.* Paris: OECD Publishing. p. 12. https://www.oecd.org/daf/ca/Managing-Risk-SOE-Sector-Asia.pdf

62   OECD. *Compendium of National Practices.* pp. 46–48.

63   *Compliance Risks: What You Don't Contain Can Hurt You.* pp. 2–3. https://www2.deloitte.com/us/en/pages/finance/articles/cfo-insights-compliance-risks.html (accessed 28 April 2021).

64   OECD. *Compendium of National Practices.* pp. 51–52.

utilities in developing economies (including India, Pakistan, Philippines, Tajikistan, and Viet Nam) reveals, however, that tariffs fully cover operating costs and the economic opportunity costs of debt and equity capital—both existing capital expenditure and new capital expenditures required to meet future demand—in only three cases. In almost half the cases, tariffs are insufficient to cover just operating expenses excluding depreciation. Operating costs and existing capital costs are covered in just over 40% of these cases.[65] A more limited survey of electricity sectors in East Asia concurs that cost recovery is "poor" in half the cases.[66] Failures to recover operating costs may lead to near-term blackouts, while insufficient recovery of capital costs may result in long-term under investment.

Recovery of costs by utilities depends on tariffs as well as other factors. In almost 90% of the cases studied, electricity tariffs are insufficient to cover all costs.[67] However, this issue may be exacerbated by the utility itself (e.g., through poor expense controls or weak collection) or by arrears arising from a failure among public sector agencies to pay their bills.[68]

Utilities that fail to cover their costs often become dependent on government handouts. In 11 of 15 jurisdictions found to be "below full cost recovery," electricity utilities "receive fiscal support in the form of operational and/or capital transfers." Though these transfers often do not cover all costs. Moreover, governments and other SOEs may also fail to pay their own electricity bills. Utilities may be forced to cope with their own arrears on payables, default, or disadvantageous borrowing, including expensive short-term debt.[69]

Full cost recovery, necessary for a utility's self-reliance and creditworthiness, can be achieved in various ways. Efficient management of costs, billing, and collections by the utility company seems a prerequisite. The evidence suggests that tariffs will be sufficient when set in a way that is technically competent and free from political interference, and that this can be done under different market models.[70]

Financial assistance, or other forms of non-commercial assistance to SOEs, may hurt competitive neutrality. This issue in Asia has been addressed by the Trans-Pacific Partnership trade agreement of 2016, which limits non-commercial assistance to SOEs, including direct payments, preferential financing, and in-kind support. The Trans-Pacific Partnership also defines favorable financing and other support: For example, below-market interest rate; a longer maturity or balloon-repayment schedule; lower collateral requirement; or less stringency by a bank (e.g., a state-owned bank) for calling loans, activating technical default or cross-default clauses, pursuing foreclosure, or initiating court-supervised bankruptcy against a financially distressed or defaulting SOE. "Equity capital inconsistent with the usual investment practice" could be interpreted to include too much equity (e.g., from too-low dividends), enabling the SOE to gain competitive advantage through acceptance of excessive risk or otherwise unsustainable losses for gain of market share; failure by the SOE shareholder to seek an adequate risk-adjusted return on its equity, with similar competitive implications; or protection of a low-performing SOE from hostile takeover.[71]

Compensation to offset public sector mandates or SOE-specific advantages is important to safeguard competitive neutrality. The compensation mechanism should be reliable and transparent, both financially and legally.

65   J. Huenteler et al. 2020. Cost Recovery and Financial Viability of the Power Sector in Developing Countries: Insights from 15 Case Studies. *Policy Research Working Paper 9136.* Washington, DC: World Bank. pp. 5, 12. https://openknowledge.worldbank.org/bitstream/handle/10986/33292/Cost-Recovery-and-Financial-Viability-of-the-Power-Sector-in-Developing-Countries-Insights-from-15-Case-Studies.pdf?sequence=1&isAllowed=y

66   World Bank. 2017. *The Status of Infrastructure Services in East Asia and the Pacific.* Washington, DC: World Bank. p. 11. http://documents1.worldbank.org/curated/en/460481511156674051/pdf/121466-REVISED-PUBLIC-EAP-Infrastructure-Status-Final-Report.pdf

67   Huenteler et al. Cost Recovery and Financial Viability of the Power Sector in Developing Countries. p. 11.

68   Huenteler et al. Cost Recovery and Financial Viability of the Power Sector in Developing Countries. pp. 11, 13–14, 17.

69   Huenteler et al. Cost Recovery and Financial Viability of the Power Sector in Developing Countries. pp. 17–18.

70   Huenteler et al. Cost Recovery and Financial Viability of the Power Sector in Developing Countries. pp. 40–41.

71   Trans-Pacific Partnership Agreement. Article 17.1. https://ustr.gov/trade-agreements/free-trade-agreements/trans-pacific-partnership/tpp-full-text

Through formal systems for "community service obligations" or "public service obligations," SOEs may be compensated for their public service mandates. In practice, such compensation may vary. However, the best approach is transparent payments from the public sector budgets to the SOE, with clear links to SOE outputs and achieving the mandate. Other methods, such as cross-subsidies from profitable to loss-making SOEs, are generally less transparent and harder to hold the SOE accountable for, and they damage the performance of the profitable SOE. SOEs should also maintain clear accounts to separate commercial activities from those carried out as part of public service obligation.[72]

Compensation for financing advantages: On debt financing for SOEs, interest rates appear to average 1.1–1.4 percentage points lower for SOE compared with private corporate borrowing (footnote 35). In the case of OECD SOEs, Australia, Estonia, Hungary, the United Kingdom (UK), and Switzerland try to ensure that loans from the government are close to market rates. In Australia, SOEs must pay a competitive neutrality fee to the government if an SOE pays lower-than-market rates on its debt. Some OECD economies also ensure that SOEs provide a minimum return on state equity investments.[73]

Competitive neutrality issues aside, differential treatment of SOEs may pose financial risks unique to SOEs. For example:
- The government may remove a differential advantage. This could include, for example, changes in tax or public procurement or a relaxed stance regarding SOE nonpayment of debt or other arrears.
- The government may impose a differential disadvantage. For example, the government could impose new or more onerous public sector mandates.
- Indeterminate compensation for public service mandates may obscure an SOE's financial performance and position. Compensation may be too little, too much, or just right. But the actual amount of compensation and underlying differential costs of a public service mandate should be clear to investors.

D.   Management Capacity

The quality of its management also significantly affects an SOE's financial performance, position, and prospects. Rating agencies have various methods for rating the quality of corporate management. For example, "Fitch considers the collective management's record in terms of its ability to create a healthy business mix, maintain operating efficiency, and strengthen...market position." In addition, "risk tolerance and consistency are important elements in the assessment (footnote 43)." For its part, S&P considers management's results, its expertise and experience, and its breadth and depth (Table 8).

---

[72]   OECD. *Compendium of National Practices.* pp. 48–50.
[73]   OECD. *Compendium of National Practices.* pp. 55–56.

Table 8: Illustrative Criteria for Management Capacity

Item	Positive	Neutral	Negative
1. Management's operational effectiveness	Management has a demonstrated history of not incurring unexpected declines in earnings or cash flow from operational risks.	Emergence of unexpected operational risks occasionally affects earnings or cash flow.	Emergence of unexpected operational risks regularly affects earnings or cash flow.
2. Management's expertise and experience	Management has considerable expertise, experience, and has a track record of success in operating all of its major lines of business.	Management has sufficient but unexceptional expertise and experience in operating its major lines of business.	Management lacks the expertise and experience to fully understand and control many of its businesses. The enterprise often deviates significantly from its plans.
3. Management's depth and breadth	Management has good depth and breadth across its major lines of business, and can withstand loss of key personnel without significant disruption to operations or cash flows in each of its significant business units.	Management depth or breadth is limited in some areas. The loss of key personnel would be expected to affect only temporarily the enterprise's operations or cash flows.	The enterprise relies on a small number of managers. The loss of key personnel would seriously affect the enterprise's operations.

Source: Standard & Poors. 2012. *Methodology: Management and Governance Credit Factors for Corporate Entities and Insurers.* New York: S&P. pp. 5–6. https://erm.ncsu.edu/az/erm/i/chan/library/SP_MandG_Methodology.pdf

E.   Corporate Governance

Corporate governance seeks to address two market imperfections. First, corporate insiders (e.g., management and directors) may pursue personal interests that differ from those of the shareholders, a principal–agent issue. Second, corporate insiders know more about a corporation's prospects and financial performance and position than do outside lenders or shareholders, an asymmetrical information problem.

Rating agencies view corporate governance as another "asymmetric consideration" for credit ratings. Good corporate governance does not increase a corporation's credit rating; however, bad corporate governance can sink it. S&P's methodology for scoring corporate governance highlights some negative factors:

* *BOD*—Insufficient independence from management may weaken oversight and encourage neglect of important risks and potential conflicts of interest.
* *Controlling shareholder*—Ownership concentration may degrade corporate decisions by emphasizing "the interests of controlling owners above those of other stakeholders."
* *Management*—Management may focus too much on its own interests.
* *Compliance*—The enterprise has a record of not complying with regulatory, tax, or legal requirements.
* *Internal controls*—Restatements or delays in financial reporting, for example, may indicate a deficient internal control environment.
* *Financial reporting and transparency*—If opaque or hides the real motivation behind certain material transactions.[74]

State ownership of an enterprise can further complicate corporate governance. Insulated from hostile takeover or bankruptcy, possibilities that discipline private corporations, SOEs may suffer from too much political interference or too little government oversight. Further complications may arise from conflict and confusion within the government over the boundary between ownership rights and regulatory rights, and between commercial

---

[74]   *S&P. Management and Governance Credit Factors.* p. 6.

performance and support for the government's economic or social agenda.[75] Finally, bureaucrats may lack familiarity with financial concepts and normal corporate governance practices, or feel conflicted between financial and social and or political goals.

Proper actions on the portfolio composition, state shareholding practices, boards of directors, and financial reporting can move SOE corporate governance toward private best practice.

Portfolio composition decisions by a government establish the extent of its responsibilities for SOE corporate governance. Privatizations involving the sale of all or a majority of state shares would decrease the number of SOEs for which the government is primarily responsible—and associated demands on government capacity. Mixed-capital arrangements, whereby varying proportions of SOEs' shares are owned by the state or by private investors, would supplement government capacity and share corporate governance responsibility with private investors. Such arrangements would also facilitate ongoing access to debt or additional equity financing from private investors. If a government's capacity to monitor SOEs' plans, initiatives, operations, and finances is particularly limited, privatization and/or mixed-capital arrangements can reduce its corporate governance burdens.

A partial public listing of SOE shares,[76] by exposing the SOE to capital market monitoring, can supplement government supervision and thereby enhance corporate governance. In the PRC during 1990–2002, the authorities packaged the better-performing assets of hundreds of SOEs into new subsidiaries, shares in which were then listed and sold—mostly on the Shanghai or Shenzhen stock exchanges. Less-desirable assets remained with preexisting SOE "parents." The retention of "non-tradable shares" in newly listed subsidiaries by state-owned or controlled institutions ensured continued state control. This approach sometimes initially disadvantaged public minority shareholders, when RPTs (e.g., borrowing) extracted cash from listed subsidiaries to support struggling SOE parents. Reforms in 2004–2005, however, then achieved "some startling results." Small percentages of shareholders were able to reject equity dilutions and RPTs at state-majority SOEs. These reforms also encouraged some SOEs to reduce corporate complexity and related parties.[77]

While opening an SOE to some capital market supervision and governance, a government may still wish to safeguard what it perceives as strategic economic interests. Governments have done this in various ways: for example, by (i) retaining majority state ownership and limiting private ownership to a minority share, (ii) maintaining a "golden share," or (iii) maintaining a "blocking minority" shareholding.

A majority state shareholding may put minority public shareholders in a disadvantageous situation, as noted earlier. Minority shareholder rights should be protected, for example, through legal entitlements to information, *pro rata* receipt of dividends, equal treatment with similarly situated shareholders, and protections in the event of new share issues or changes in control. Procedures to bolster minority shareholders' representation on SOE boards for example, through cumulative voting whereby shareholders may cast all of their votes for a single director nominee—may also be desirable.[78] Protections against RPTs are discussed later.

A golden share in a company allows the government to block major decisions it disagrees with, including takeovers by foreign companies or owners. For example, when the British Airports Authority was privatized in 1987, the UK

---

[75]   OECD. *OECD Guidelines on Corporate Governance of State-Owned Enterprises.* p. 12.

[76]   A partial public listing of SOE shares (footnote 5), by exposing the SOE to capital market monitoring, can supplement government supervision and thereby enhance corporate governance..

[77]   W. P. Mako and C. Zhang. 2008. Why Is China So Different from Other Transition Economies? In I. W. Lieberman and D. J. Kopf, eds. *Privatization in Transition Economies: The Ongoing Story.* New York: Elsevier. pp. 183–184, 189–190, 196–200.

[78]   For more detailed suggestions on the protection of minority shareholders, see World Bank. 2014. *Corporate Governance of State-Owned Enterprises: A Toolkit.* Washington, DC: World Bank. pp. 248–252. https://openknowledge.worldbank.org/bitstream/handle/10986/20390/9781464802225.pdf?sequence=1&isAllowed=y

government retained a golden share. UK practice then spread to other European countries and Brazil.[79] Since 2003, European Union courts have disallowed golden shares as a constraint on the free movement of capital.[80] But they are still found outside of the European Union.

A blocking minority shareholding takes advantage of any requirement in a country's company law or a corporation's articles, requiring a supermajority of voting shares to approve certain corporate actions. Such corporate actions include, for example, liquidation, equity dilution, a merger, or corporate acquisition above some size threshold, or movement of the corporation's domicile to a foreign country. For example, an early 1990s debt crisis led to revision of the legal mandate for Austria's OIAG state shareholding fund. Its 1993 governing law required OIAG to sell its majority holdings in Austrian SOEs to pay down debt, while stipulating that OIAG's shareholdings should not go below the level (25% + 1 share) needed under Austria's company law to block fundamental changes in a company's business or capital structure. Thus, as of April 2020, a successor state shareholding fund (OBAG) retained blocking minorities in two SOEs: oil refiner OMV (31.5%) and Telekom Austria (28.4%).[81]

Effective corporate governance then hinges on balancing autonomy versus oversight. This is required both between shareholders and the SOE board as well as between the SOE board and management. Such balance is important regardless of the mix of state versus private ownership.

An autonomy-oversight imbalance creates risk. With too little autonomy, the board or SOE management may be unable to respond to changing market conditions. However, too little oversight raises the risk of imprudent investment and financing decisions that can result in financial loss for the shareholder(s).

A desirable division of labor for the corporate governance of SOEs is as follows:
- As owner, the state establishes its overall "expectations" of SOEs and sets mandates or broad objectives for the SOEs it oversees.
- The BOD sets the strategy for achieving the mandates or objectives, oversees the management, and monitors performance.
- The management is responsible for implementing the strategy and is accountable to the board.[82]

State shareholding practices provide the foundation for good corporate governance of SOEs. The state shareholding function is often the trickiest aspect of SOE corporate governance. Governments and SOEs may find it easier to implement some semblance of board governance than to achieve a proper autonomy-oversight balance between state shareholder and SOE.

Best-practice principles for state shareholders are well established. OECD guidelines indicate, for example, that the state shareholder should remain informed, while the SOEs should have autonomy to achieve their mandate and objectives. In addition, SOE boards should also be allowed to carry out their functions without meddling from the state or political interference. They should remain accountable.[83]

[79] R. Dhir. Golden Share. *Investopedia.* updated 6 May 2020. https://www.investopedia.com/terms/g/goldenshare.asp#:~:text=A%20golden%20 share%20is%20a,a%20ratio%20of%20ordinary%20shares

[80] BAA 'Golden Share' Ruled Illegal. *BBC News.* 13 May 2003. http://news.bbc.co.uk/2/hi/business/3022809.stm ; and Court of Justice of the European Union. 2010. Portugal's Holding of Golden Shares in Energies de Portugal is Contrary to European Union Law. Press release. 11 November. https://ec.europa.eu/commission/presscorner/detail/en/CJE_10_112

[81] For example, OIAG reduced its shareholdings in the Boehler Udenholm steel SOE from 73% in 1994 to 25% in 1996. Mako and Zhang. Exercising Ownership Rights in State-Owned Enterprise Groups. p. 9.

[82] World Bank. *Corporate Governance of State-Owned Enterprises.* p. 179.

[83] OECD. *OECD Guidelines on Corporate Governance of State-Owned Enterprises.* pp. 18, 26. For additional principles and more details on state ownership, see Chapter II "The State's Role as an Owner," pp. 18–19, and Annotations to Chapter II, pp. 33–44.

State shareholding models vary widely, both globally and across Asia. Within Asia, some jurisdictions (e.g., Cambodia and Pakistan) take a decentralized approach, while others (e.g., Republic of Korea and Singapore) have centralized the state ownership function in one institution (Table 9).

Table 9: State Shareholding Models for Selected Asian Countries

Model	Model characteristics	Selected countries
Decentralized	No one single institution or state actor acts on the responsibilities of the ownership function. Public perception often perceives line-ministries to be de facto running the SOE as an extension of their ministerial powers. For each of the three ownership function responsibilities, a unique state unit or a mix of state units subsumes the role.	Cambodia and Pakistan
Decentralized, with a coordinating agency	Specialized government units act in an advisory capacity to other shareholding ministries on technical and operational issues, and their most important mandate often is to monitor SOE performance. The more limited role of these central agencies, coupled with the autonomy that line ministries thus maintain, leads to considerable overlap with the decentralized model.	India, Philippines, and Viet Nam
Dual model	Two government institutions—often one line-ministry per SOE plus the finance ministry—share the ownership function for each SOE. Typically, the finance ministry sets financial objectives, while the other formulates operational strategy.	Indonesia
Centralized, with exceptions	As provided later, with exceptions	Bhutan, Kazakhstan, Malaysia, and People's Republic of China
Centralized	One government institution carries out the mission as a shareholder in all companies and organizations controlled by the state. This institution can be a designated government ministry, specialized ownership agency, or state shareholding fund. Financial targets, technical and operational issues, and monitoring of SOE performance are all conducted by the central body. Board members are appointed in different ways but the instrumental input comes from the central unit.	Republic of Korea and Singapore

Sources: OECD. *Compendium of National Practices.* 24; and OECD. 2020. *Transparency Frameworks for State-Owned Enterprises in Asia* Paris: OECD Publishing. p. 12. https://www.oecd.org/corporate/ca/Transparency-Frameworks-Asia-2020.pdf; and David Robinett, personal correspondence.

Per best practice, "the exercise of ownership rights should be centralized in a single ownership entity." This could include a first-tier government entity (e.g., a ministry or ownership agency) or a second-tier state-shareholding fund (likely owned by its ministry of finance). A "coordinating body" would be the next-best alternative. In either case, "this 'ownership entity' should have the capacity and competencies to effectively carry out its duties."[84]

Centralization of the state ownership function offers important advantages. Such centralization serves several objectives: "To separate the state's ownership functions from its policy-making and regulatory or supervisory functions to help avoid or minimize potential conflicts of interest. To minimize the scope for political interference and bring greater professionalism to the state's ownership role by pooling specialized capabilities and scarce resources. To promote greater coherence and consistency in applying corporate governance standards and in exercising the state's ownership role across all SOEs."[85]

The state shareholder should rely on "normal" corporate governance methods. To avoid interference with management and respect board independence, which can easily become issues for SOEs, the state shareholder should follow private sector norms in limiting its engagement to the following: (i) attending shareholder meetings and voting the state's shares; (ii) setting up a merit-based process for board nomination and appointment; and

---

[84]   OECD. *OECD Guidelines on Corporate Governance of State-Owned Enterprises.* p. 18.
[85]   World Bank. *Corporate Governance of State-Owned Enterprises.* p. 78. For a more detailed discussion of alternative state ownership arrangements and implementation issues, see Chapter 3, "State Ownership Arrangements," pp. 69–98.

(iii) monitoring board and SOE performance. In addition, the state shareholder should ensure that SOE reporting systems and disclosure are adequate, and that board compensation can attract qualified candidates.[86]

Boards of directors—positioned between shareholders and management—play a pivotal role in corporate governance, including for SOEs. Key issues pertain to board composition, responsibility and authority, organization, operation, and remuneration. Management of conflicts of interest, including from RPTs, should be a key responsibility.

Board composition should promote board independence. Consistent with the private sector rating agency criteria, the board should maintain "sufficient independence from management to provide effective oversight of it." In addition, it is important to offset the influence of controlling shareholders—often an issue for SOEs.[87] This should include independent board members from the private sector. Directors from the private sector can offer independence, as well as the experience and perspective to enhance oversight. Thus, by 2014, many OECD countries had reduced government representatives and increased the number of independent directors on SOE boards. In some countries, such as Australia and Sweden, almost all SOE board members are independent. In the Republic of Korea, "a majority of directors have to be independent, including the chair." Meanwhile, "India and Malaysia stipulate that independent directors make up at least a third of the board in SOEs," and "Indonesia calls for a 25 percent share."[88]

Director appointments should follow a structured nomination process designed to enhance board professionalism and independence to support effective oversight of SOE management. This process would usefully include the "adoption of professional criteria for selection and dismissal of directors" and objective assessment of board skills, both existing and missing. Politics should not play a role. "To reduce ministerial influence, a number of countries therefore have adopted governance reforms that delegate part or all of the nomination process to an advisory body, centralized ownership entity, or the SOEs themselves." For example, "in Malaysia the nomination committee of listed SOEs identifies potential board candidates (in conjunction with Khazanah [state shareholding fund] and others), prepares a short list for approval by the board, and then submits the approved list to Khazanah for appointment." An "independent [SOE] nomination committee chaired by an independent director and consisting only of nonexecutive directors" would promote professionalism. Development of a pool of prequalified director candidates can also facilitate nominations.[89]

A board's primary responsibilities are to oversee strategy and management, and monitor the corporation's performance. An SOE's strategy should be in in-line with its mandate, broad objectives, and necessary service delivery requirements.[90] Making the CEO clearly responsible to the board would tend to reduce the scope for political interference in SOE initiatives and focus responsibility on the board. More particularly, OECD guidelines recommend that "SOE boards should actively (i) formulate or approve, monitor and review corporate strategy, within the framework of the overall corporate objectives; (ii) establish appropriate performance indicators and identify key risks; (iii) develop and oversee effective risk management policies and procedures with respect to financial and operational risks, but also with respect to human rights, labor, environmental and tax-related issues; (iv) monitor disclosure and communication processes, ensuring that the financial statements fairly present the affairs of the SOE and reflect the risks incurred; (v) assess and monitor management performance; and (vi) decide

---

[86]   OECD. *OECD Guidelines on Corporate Governance of State-Owned Enterprises.* pp. 18–19.

[87]   S&P. *Management and Governance Credit Factors.* p. 6.

[88]   World Bank. *Corporate Governance of State-Owned Enterprises.* pp. 164, 166, 168. For broader and more detailed discussion of board composition, see pp. 160–169.

[89]   World Bank. *Corporate Governance of State-Owned Enterprises.* pp. 169, 172–173, 175, 177. For a more thorough and illustrated discussion of structured nomination processes, see pp. 172–179.

[90]   OECD. *OECD Guidelines on Corporate Governance of State-Owned Enterprises.* p. 26.

on CEO remuneration and develop effective succession plans for key executives."[91] To facilitate financial and operational risk management, the board should ensure that the SOE develops "efficient internal audit procedures and [establishes] an internal audit function that is monitored and directly reports to the board."[92]

Thus, Australia, Germany, New Zealand, Norway, Sweden, and a growing number of other countries leave CEO selection to the board, not the government. In turn, managers are chosen by the CEO, with some input from the board, depending on standard practice in the jurisdiction.[93] *This promotes a continuum of responsibility: from management team to the CEO, the CEO to the board, and the board to the shareholder(s).*

An important board responsibility is to protect shareholders from harm due to conflicts of interest, including RPTs. Independent board members should have minimal conflicts of interest, involving the enterprise, the management or major shareholders, including the government. In addition, "mechanisms should be implemented to avoid conflicts of interest preventing board members from objectively carrying out their board duties and to limit political interference in board processes" (footnote 90). Conflicts may be commercial—"in which a board member, a manager, or one of their relatives has an interest in a contract or a transaction with the SOE, either directly or through, for example, ownership in another company"—or political—"in which a government representative pursues a policy goal contrary to the interests of the SOE." In such situations, "the standard approach is to declare that conflict to the board, abstain from voting on the matter involved, and in some cases, abstain from participating in a board discussion on the matter." Other potential conflicts include the use of privileged information in a private transaction "to the detriment of the company" or in securities trading. "Many countries now require that SOEs have a code of ethics or conduct that applies to the board and other employees."[94]

Similar procedures are recommended to control RPTs. Misuse of SOE assets can hurt financial performance and position, as noted in Section III.A. "Transactions in which board members, management, or influential shareholders have a conflict of interest are prone to abuse."[95] Contracts, loans, or property sales to such related parties are an easy way to siphon assets away from an SOE, hurting its shareholders. Most guidance on RPTs requires disclosure, and approval by disinterested and independent board members. In some jurisdictions, only disinterested shareholders—usually those that are not the controlling shareholder—may approve an (RPT) before it takes place. Rules such as these may be established as statutory requirements for all SOEs or may be part of the articles for specific SOEs."[96]

The World Bank's *SOE Toolkit*[97] usefully addresses other key aspects of SOE board governance, including organization of specialized board committees, such as for audit and nominations (192–196), formal procedures for board operations (191–192), board remuneration (196–202), board evaluation (202–203), and director training (203–205).

Financial statements should be meaningful, accurate, and clear for investors. SOEs "should observe high standards of transparency and be subject to the same high-quality accounting, disclosure, compliance, and auditing standards as listed companies."[98] This corresponds to International Financial Reporting Standards (IFRS) for accounting. Regarding audits, "specific state control procedures do not substitute for an independent external audit" of SOEs'

---

91   OECD. *OECD Guidelines on Corporate Governance of State-Owned Enterprises.* p. 70.
92   OECD. *OECD Guidelines on Corporate Governance of State-Owned Enterprises.* p. 27.
93   World Bank. *Corporate Governance of State-Owned Enterprises.* pp. 187–188. For more on the definition and implementation of board responsibilities, including on optimal board size and separation of the chair from the CEO, see pp. 179–189.
94   World Bank. *Corporate Governance of State-Owned Enterprises.* pp. 184–185.
95   World Bank. *Corporate Governance of State-Owned Enterprises.* p. 252.
96   World Bank. *Corporate Governance of State-Owned Enterprises.* p. 253.
97   World Bank. *Corporate Governance of State-Owned Enterprises.*
98   OECD. *OECD Guidelines on Corporate Governance of State-Owned Enterprises.* p. 24.

financial statements. "An independent external audit [should be] based on high-quality standards" (footnote 98), such as International Accounting Standards (IAS).

These requirements, perhaps more easily said than done, are essential. A major corporate governance weakness in many countries is the poor quality of financial reporting and auditing, including from noncompliance with IFRS (where applied) or local accounting standards; long delays in preparation and publication of financial statements; failures to address noncompliance qualifications in audit reports; and insufficient professional capacity to apply IFRS and IAS. A resulting lack of financial statement reliability may mask serious financial distress, impede informed decision-making by managers and directors, and preclude any international credit rating.[99] Mitigation of such shortcomings may require support from international partners to help implement IFRS and IAS and train local accounting and audit professionals.

The public (i.e., non-private) nature of SOEs may well require more fulsome disclosures. This would include disclosure of policy mandates and other activities encouraged or required by the government. Other information to disclose "include (1) a clear statement of...enterprise objectives and their fulfillment (for fully-owned SOEs this would include any mandate elaborated by the state ownership entity); (2) enterprise financial and operating results, including where relevant the costs and funding arrangements pertaining to public policy objectives; (3) the governance, ownership and voting structure of the enterprise, including the content of any corporate governance and implementation processes; (4) the remuneration of board members and key executives; (5) board member qualifications, selection process, including board diversity policies, roles on other company boards and whether they are considered as independent by the SOE board; (6) any material foreseeable risk factors and measures taken to manage such risks; (7) any financial assistance, including guarantees, received from the state and commitments made on behalf of the SOE, including contractual commitments and liabilities arising from public-private partnerships; (8) any material transactions with the state and other related entities; (9) any relevant issues relating to employees and other stakeholders" (footnote 96).

Finally, the foregoing should be disclosed to the public. This includes through government, ownership entity, and SOE websites.[100]

---

[99]   Srinivasan Janardanam, ADB, private correspondence, 21 January 2021.
[100]   OECD. *OECD Guidelines on Corporate Governance of State-Owned Enterprises.* p. 25.

V. Additional Resources

A round 35 development finance institutions (DFIs), including ADB, as well as other MDBs and bilateral donors and export credit agencies, have adopted a Corporate Governance Development Framework (CGDF) for use in their investment processes. This CGDF represents a distillation of the World Bank Group's International Finance Corporation methodology for evaluating corporate governance risks and opportunities.

Extensive collaboration among signatories of the DFI Working Group on Corporate Governance produced, in 2010, an agreed DFI Toolkit on Corporate Governance. This toolkit is intended to provide a common basis for (i) assessing the corporate governance of DFI investee companies and (ii) achieving faster progress in implementation of the CGDF.

The DFI Toolkit on Corporate Governance includes (i) a Corporate Governance Questionnaire and (ii) a Corporate Governance Progression Matrix. It also provides instructions, definitions of key terms, and sample documents. These are available via the following links:
- Corporate Governance Questionnaire
- Corporate Governance Progression Matrix
- Corporate Governance Instruction Sheet
- List of Key Corporate Governance Terms
- Sample – Corporate Governance Improvement Program
- Sample – Corporate Governance Section in Internal Approval Documents.

Finally, DFI signatories to the CGDF typically maintain active advisory units that advise counterpart governments and SOE boards on corporate governance improvements, as well as on economic management, financial development, and governance enhancements.

Appendix

Suggested Guidelines for Assessing Risk in the Commercial Financing of State-Owned Enterprises

Item	Responsibility	Best practice	Good practice	Marginal
A. Financial Performance & Resilience				
Corporate credit rating[a]	State shareholder, Board and management	• SOE's credit rated by multiple rating agencies as investment grade (e.g., AAA, AA, A, or BBB)		• SOE's credit rated by multiple rating agencies as "highly speculative" (e.g., BB)
Leverage	Board and management	• Projected cash flow and debt ratios above industry average	• Projected cash flow and debt ratios at industry average	• Projected cash flow and debt ratios below industry average
Additional financial flexibility	Board and management	• Rapid ability to revise capital spending plans; • Sought after as a banking client; • Ready access to international and domestic debt and equity markets; • Committed long-dated credit lines; and • Below-average proportion of short-term debt	• Some ability to revise capital spending plans; • Good banking relationships; • Able to access international and domestic debt and equity markets; • Committed credit lines; and • Average proportion of short-term debt	• Low flexibility in capital spending plans; • Limited banking relationships; • Uncertain access to international and domestic debt and equity markets; • Lack of credit lines; • Above-average proportion of short-term debt
Returns on equity (ROE)	Board and management	• ROE above industry average	• ROE at industry average	• ROE below industry average
B. Business & Risk Management				
Corporate complexity	Board	• Noncomplex group structure; • Transparent reporting	• Group structure has some complexity, but mitigated by transparent reporting	• Complex group structure or nontransparent ownership structure; • Related-party transactions (RPTs) occur, but have a reasonable economic rationale
Strategic planning process	Board and management	• Evidence of strategic planning, with specific financial and operational goals, including clear measures of achievement	• Strategic plans, but insufficient depth or specificity in operational and financial goals and performance indicators	• Limited evidence of systematic strategic planning, or superficial planning. • Decisions ad hoc and opportunistic
Strategy realism	Board and management	• Strategy nearly always consistent with enterprise capabilities, considering market conditions. • Have a track record of market leadership and effective innovation	• Strategy generally consistent with enterprise capabilities, considering market conditions	• Strategy inconsistent with enterprise capabilities or market conditions. • Abrupt or frequent changes in strategy, acquisitions, divestitures, or restructuring

continued on next page

continued

Item	Responsibility	Best practice	Good practice	Marginal
Strategy plementation	Management	• Management has been able to convert nearly all strategic decisions into constructive action • Has a track record of achieving financial and operational goals • Successful relative to peers	• Management has been able to convert most strategic decisions into constructive action • Has a track record of achieving most operational and financial goals	• Management is often unable to convert strategic decisions into constructive action. • Often fails to achieve its operational and financial goals
Risk management	Board and management	• Management has successfully implemented comprehensive policies that effectively identify, monitor, select, and mitigate key risks • Tolerances articulated to shareholders	• A basic set of standards in place, but may lack fully developed risk management capabilities	• No or few defined standards and tolerances, and little risk management capability
Operational control	Management	• Rigorous and ambitious (but reasonable) standards for operational performance, regularly monitored	• Standards for operational performance, regularly monitored, are achievable and similar to industry norms	• Management lacks the capacity, discipline, or commitment to achieve set standards, or sets low standards
C. Country & Government Risk				
Economic environment	Government	• Very stable; major advanced economy; high resilience to economic shocks	• Moderately stable economy; could be less advanced, but with resilience to economic shocks	• Less stable, less advanced economy; still susceptible to adverse changes in domestic situation or international shocks
Financial development	Government	• Consistent implementation and supervision of Financial Stability Board (FSB) standards; banking sector very developed, with high-entry barriers; very advanced financial markets	• Some gaps in the implementation or supervision of FSB standards; banking sector less developed, with only moderate-entry barriers; and financial markets developed but not deep	• Substantial gaps in the implementation or supervision of FSB standards; banking sector diffuse, with only limited entry barriers; and financial markets not fully developed
Governance	Government	• Weighted average of World Bank's Worldwide Governance indicators in the top 20%	• Weighted average of World Bank's Worldwide Governance indicators in the top 30%–500%	• Weighted average of World Bank's Worldwide Governance indicators in the top 60%
Utility regulation	Government	• Full economic cost recovery	• Full economic cost recovery	• Full recovery of operating costs and current opportunity costs of debt and equity capital
Regulation of SOEs	Government	• Equal or similar regulation as for private businesses, except perhaps for natural monopolies	• Equal or similar regulation as for private businesses (except perhaps for natural monopolies), but with regulatory preferences to compensate for public service obligations	• Relative to private businesses, significantly more or less stringent regulation of SOEs
Taxation of SOEs	Government	• Same as for private firms	• Largely similar as for private firms	• Significant advantages or disadvantages for SOEs
Compliance	Board and management	• Per minimal standard	• Per minimal standard	• SOE remains generally free of regulatory, tax or legal infractions; has stable relations with government authorities

continued on next page

continued

Item	Responsibility	Best practice	Good practice	Marginal
Access to finance	Government and state financial institutions	• Per minimal standard	• Per minimal standard	• No differential access to finance based on SOE status
Public service mandates	Government	• No requirement for SOE to undertake non-commercial activities for public purposes	• Some public service mandates • But subject to complete and clear rules • SOE receives direct compensation	• More significant public service mandates • Incomplete rules • SOE receives some compensation, for which basis is unclear
Competitive neutrality	Government	• Not applicable (no public service mandates)	• Clear rules and mechanism for SOE to pay or receive compensation for all demonstrable benefits or costs from regulatory, tax, or public service mandate differences based on SOE status	• Some rules and mechanism for compensation for some benefits or costs from regulatory, tax, or public service mandate differences based on SOE status
D. Management				
Operational effectiveness	Management	• A demonstrated history of not incurring unexpected declines in earnings or cash flow	• Emergence of unexpected operational risks occasionally affects earnings or cash flow	• Emergence of unexpected operational risks regularly affects earnings or cash flow
Expertise and experience	Board and management	• Considerable expertise, experience and a track record of success in operating all of its major lines of business	• Sufficient but unexceptional expertise and experience in operating its major lines of business	• Insufficient expertise and experience to fully understand and control many of its businesses • SOE often deviates significantly from its plans
Depth breadth	Management	• Management has good depth and breadth across its major lines of business, and can withstand loss of key personnel without significant disruption to operations or cash flows in each of its significant business units	• Management depth or breadth is limited in some areas. • The loss of key personnel would be expected to affect only temporarily the SOE's operations or cash flows	• The SOE relies on a small number of managers • The loss of key personnel would seriously affect the SOE's operations
E. Corporate Governance				
Designation of State shareholder	Government	• The government has designated one ministry, agency, or fund as the State shareholder for most or all SOEs. • The designated state shareholder is responsible for SOEs' performance	• The government has designated more than one entity as State shareholder for SOEs • Responsibility split among state shareholders	• Decentralized; other than "the government," no official or entity is clearly responsible for SOE performance
	State shareholder	• Per minimal standard	• Per minimal standard	• The state shareholder remains regularly informed about each SOE • The state shareholder interacts with the SOE board through "normal" shareholder channels (i.e., shareholder meetings and voting), but does not otherwise intervene

continued on next page

continued

Item	Responsibility	Best practice	Good practice	Marginal
Equity mix	Government	• State ownership in the SOE is limited to a minority share sufficient to block major corporate developments (e.g., liquidation, equity dilution and change in national domicile)	• The state owns a majority of shares, but the public shareholding is sufficient to block a major corporate action (e.g., M&A transaction) • The influence of controlling shareholders is offset by risk-aware professional management, while the board effectively serves the interest of all shareholders	• An SOE has some public shareholders, but not enough to block a major corporate decision (e.g., M&A transaction)
Treatment of minority shareholders	Government and board	• The state has no special rights (e.g., golden share) beyond its ownership • A super-majority of shareholders must approve major corporate developments • Rights of shareholders are protected during new-share issues and changes of control, including privatizations and re-nationalizations • Rules on RPTs address transactions with the government and other SOEs and require recusal by interested shareholders • Effective board representation of minority shareholders is provided through cumulative voting or similar mechanisms • Minority shareholders can ask questions at a shareholders' meeting and influence its agenda • Information is disclosed equally to all securities holders	• Shareholders are provided with accurate and timely information on the number of shares held by the state and other major shareholders • The board encourages minority shareholders to participate in shareholders meetings • Minority shareholders may nominate board members	• The SOE's legal framework treats all shareholders of the same class equally with respect to voting rights, subscription rights, and transfer rights • Minority shareholders participate in the shareholder's meeting and receive dividends • Changing the SOE's articles of incorporation requires super-majority approval by shareholders

continued on next page

continued

Item	Responsibility	Best practice	Good practice	Marginal
Board of Directors	State shareholder and/or board	• The board has a significant number of formally independent directors, preferably with most from the private sector • The board selects the SOE's CEO and sets CEO pay • The board ensures the integrity of financial reporting, internal control and audit, and risk management systems • The positions of Board Chair and CEO are separate • The board's audit committee composed primarily of independent directors, oversees internal controls, and audit • Board committees with independent directors oversee such areas as board compensation, nomination, and conflicts of interest. • All directors receive induction and ongoing training • The board conducts formal evaluations of itself, individual directors and the CEO	• The board includes nonexecutive directors from the private sector • The board oversees SOE management, strategy, budgets and major expenditures, etc.; the state's role in approving or guiding these matters leaves sufficient autonomy to the board • The board has a code of ethics (or conduct) and manages potential conflicts of interest among directors • The board follows written policies and procedures • A Board audit committee includes 1+ independent director • Directors' pay is linked to responsibilities • Directors have received some training	• The board includes nonexecutive directors with commercial and financial experience • No ministers or elected officials serve on the Board • The board maintains sufficient independence from management to oversee it effectively • The board oversees key SOE management activities; the state's role in approving or guiding key activities is clear • Directors seek to avoid conflicts of interest and declare them to the board • The board meets regularly, and directors understand their tasks, duties, and responsibilities • Directors receive adequate and timely information • The board is not so large as to hinder effective deliberation • Management is responsive to all stakeholders' interests, appropriately balances those, communicates consistently to all, and acknowledges the board's authority
Financial discipline: ROE targets	State shareholder, board	• State shareholder sets ROE targets, based on industry norms, in consultation with board	• Board sets ROE targets, in consultation with state shareholder	• Irregular board consideration of ROE targets
Dividend policy		• Initiative by state shareholder in providing multi-year target or guidelines for establishing dividends based on business, its optimum capital structure, and industry norms	• Board recommends multi-year targets or guidelines for establishing dividends based on business, its optimum capital structure, and industry norms	• Dividends negotiated annually between state shareholder and board
Conflicts and related-party transactions (RPTs)	Government and/or board	• Board discussion and voting on a RPT are limited to disinterested independent directors. • Approved RPTs publicly disclosed • Code of ethics	• A majority of disinterested and independent directors must approve any RPT; public disclosure • Code of ethics	• All potential RPTs are reviewed by the board. A majority of disinterested directors must approve of any RPT, which then is publicly disclosed • A code of ethics governs the disclosure and management of conflicts of interest

continued on next page

continued

Item	Responsibility	Best practice	Good practice	Marginal
Financial controls and transparency	Board and management	• The design of internal controls systems complies with the 2013 COSO (Committee of Sponsoring Organization) Integrated Framework • The internal audit unit meets the standards of the Institute of Internal Auditors, and its recommendations are taken into account • Financial statements follow International Financial Reporting Standards (IFRS) • The independent external audit is overseen by the board's audit committee, or equivalent body • The independent external auditor provides an unqualified audit opinion on the financial statements • Criteria are established for disclosing RPTs with other SOEs or with the government • Annual reports include the following: indirect ownership and control, any special voting rights, code of ethics, key performance indicators, compliance with corporate governance code, and management and Board remuneration • Annual reports gives an account on: risk management; performance against key performance indicators; environmental and social reporting; and board attendance, training, and evaluations • The SOE reports on public service or policy obligations, the costs and funding of which are fully disclosed • All public disclosure is available on the SOE and relevant government website	• The costs of meeting any policy objectives are valued using internationally accepted techniques and disclosed separately in the financial statements • The SOE's financial statements separately report the impact of any non-commercial assistance, for example, concessionary funding • Internal controls and internal audit unit are in place, staffed and adequately resourced • Risk management is part of the internal control framework • The internal audit unit is accountable to the board • The SOE prepares semi-annual financial statements per national financial reporting standards • The independent external audit follows International Standards on Auditing • The SOE acts on issues raised by the independent external auditor • Annual reports include management discussion and analysis, SOE objectives, ownership and control information, summaries of risks and RPTs, and basic details on board directors • Annual reports are publicly available	• The SOE's commercial and any policy objectives are explicit, and disclosed to the public • Funding costs and sources are transparent • Bank financing is procured competitively • Internal controls exist, receive periodic review, and are considered as not deficient • An internal audit function is in place • The state audit institution's work is clearly defined • Accounting choices reflect the economics of the business • The SOE prepares timely annual financial statements according to national financial reporting standards • Annual financial statements are audited by an independent external auditor • The SOE prepares an annual report

Sources: World Bank. *Corporate Governance of State-Owned Enterprises*. 338–341; Fitch. *Corporate Rating Criteria*. pp. 70, 75; Standard & Poors. *Management and Governance Credit Factors for Corporate Entities and Insurers*. 5–6; and Section IV discussion and references.

[a] A state-owned enterprise (SOE) should obtain multiple credit ratings from international credit rating agencies. The following items are suggestive of criteria for credit ratings of varying quality: In lieu of a credit rating from a credit rating agency, an SOE's overall attractiveness as a candidate for non-sovereign commercial credit would depend on the preponderance of ratings for individual items. The weighting among individual items might shift as cumulative perceptions of the SOE's performance and practices improve or deteriorate. As appropriate, lower rated criteria may also apply to higher ratings.

www.ingramcontent.com/pod-product-compliance
Lightning Source LLC
Chambersburg PA
CBHW050056220326

41599CB00045B/7435

* 9 7 8 9 2 9 2 6 9 0 1 2 0 *